Pilates

rd

LEARNING SUPPORT SERVICES

Please return on or before the last date stamped below

City College NORWICH

In ten session
in twenty you'
in thirty you'll

Pilates
The Way Forward

Lynne Robinson
& Gordon Thomson

PAN BOOKS

First published 1999 by Pan Books
an imprint of Macmillan Publishers Ltd
25 Eccleston Place, London SW1W 9NF
Basingstoke and Oxford
Associated companies throughout the world
www.macmillan.co.uk

ISBN 0 330 37081 2

9 8

A CIP catalogue record for this book is available from
the British Library.

Designed by Macmillan General Books Design Department
Photography by Lesley Howling
Technical illustrations by Raymond Turvey (except p.3 (bottom right),
p.18 (top right), p.20 (top right), p.21, p.55, p.69, p.96 (bottom), p144
by Cath Knox, and p.7 (bottom left), p26, p.78 by Debbie Hinks)
Typeset by SX Composing DTP, Rayleigh, Essex
Printed by Mackays of Chatham plc, Chatham, Kent.

Advice to the Reader

Before following any advice contained in this book, it is recommended
that you consult your doctor if you suffer from any health problems or
special conditions or are in any doubt as to its suitability.

Contents

Key
(I)   Intermediate level
(A)   Advanced level

Acknowledgements

Gordon

I am very grateful to Lynne for giving me the discipline to make the progression, together, towards our new book.

Also my thanks to Gordon Wise, Sarah Bennie and Neil Lang of Pan Macmillan for the confidence they have shown in our technique. As ever, to my mum and dad – especially this year during their 50th wedding anniversary – and to my loyal and supportive clients old and new, many thanks.

Lynne

Where do I start? The only reason we have been able to develop Body Control Pilates through the books, the videos and the teacher training programme, is because it seems to have a special effect on everyone it touches.

I am constantly amazed at the level of commitment and the pure energy everyone involved with our projects shows. My thanks to Gordon of course. The Body Control Pilates Association's member teachers in the UK and overseas; the teaching staff on the teaching training courses, especially Neil, Paul, Miranda, Mitsi and Sasha; the students on those courses; the team at Pan Macmillan; the boys from Telstar Video who have released the videos; our literary agent Michael Alcock; everyone working on the magazine and the clothing; Helen teaching with me here in Sevenoaks; Judy, Ellena and Cheryl at the studio; Jenny who keeps the show on the road in the office; Eva handling the PR for the clothing and the Association; Chris and Kate at IAG; and Shelley and Ian – we have now become a large, happy family and without everyone's support and endless enthusiasm we would be nowhere. A big thank you to all of you!

A special thank you, too, to our consulting physiotherapist, who is also my shopping and disco partner . . . Jacks!

And then, the biggest thanks of all to my family, my daughters Rebecca and Emily who continue to put up with me, and Leigh, who works incessantly behind the scenes to ensure that I survive and that Body Control Pilates continues to flourish.

Finally, on a professional and personal note, Gordon and I both owe a huge debt to Helge Fisher who not only works tirelessly to maintain the highest standards in everything we do together, but who is a fabulous friend.

About the Authors

Lynne Robinson and Gordon Thomson are recognized leaders and innovators in the Pilates Method of exercise. With Helge Fisher (*The Mind–Body Workout*, Pan), they established the Body Control Pilates Teacher Training partnership, now Europe's foremost Pilates training organization, graduates of which are today teaching worldwide. Lynne and Gordon are elected directors of the Body Control Pilates Association.

Alongside her media work, Lynne Robinson runs a Pilates practice in Sevenoaks, Kent, where she works closely with specialist practitioners and sports injury clinics. She has pioneered the way in developing mat-based exercises, allowing Pilates to be followed outside the traditional studio environment.

Gordon Thomson was previously an actor/dancer with Ballet Rambert and other leading companies. He has taught Pilates for twenty-three years. He is proprietor of the Body Control Pilates Studio in South Kensington, London.

Foreword

Analysis of movement is fundamental in determining why injuries occur and why the body is in pain. When the body is in perfect alignment and the muscles are working in a co-ordinated way, 'normal movement' can then occur, which is both flowing and free of pain.

As a physiotherapist who specializes in spinal pain and sports injuries, I see, on a daily basis, that any disruption to this normal movement almost inevitably leads to overuse injuries, dysfunction and pain. When this happens, the body adapts itself and learns to move in an abnormal way with the pain persisting. This is precisely why Pilates is so important and so effective. It corrects the use of faulty movement by getting right down to the core of the problem – the spine. With Pilates, people learn once again how to move correctly, by engaging the deep postural muscles.

Since introducing the Pilates Method to my patients, I have found that they maintain the improvement they have gained as a result of treatment and do not require follow-up sessions. Pilates is clearly the way forward for the prevention of pain and for feeling good in mind, body and spirit.

I can wholeheartedly recommend this book to all who exercise, to all who work in the field of rehabilitation and exercise and, especially, to all who do not yet do any exercise at all!

Why? Quite simply, Pilates is *the* way forward . . .

Jacqueline Knox MCSP, SRP
Chartered and State Registered
Physiotherapist
PostGrad ManipTher.

Why Did We Write This Book?

It is hard for us to believe that it was just two years ago that our first book *Body Control: The Pilates Way* was published. As the first ever book on the Pilates Method to be geared to the general public, it has received an enormous amount of press coverage throughout the world. What followed both amazed and delighted us: there isn't a Pilates teacher in the country who is not inundated with actual and potential clients, while the Body Control Pilates Association (which supports teachers in the areas of business and professional development) received over 12,000 enquiries in the first year alone and our teacher training programme is fully subscribed up to twelve months ahead. It is interesting to note that over half of those now training are physiotherapists, osteopaths or chiropractors!

The launch of the *Body Control: The Pilates Way* video, which was produced in association with Telstar and GMTV, was the icing on the cake. It quickly went to the Number 2 spot in the national best-seller charts, and was even hot on the heels of *The X-Files* for a period! Within the space of twelve months, Pilates had gone from relative obscurity to being *the* fitness programme — with, reassuringly, growing support from the world of medicine.

The success of the first video led to *The Pilates Weekly Workout* being released in December 1998 with, once again, an equivalent sales success and we have also succeeded in keeping the printing presses rolling with *The Mind–Body Workout* and *Pilates Through the Day* — a series of mini bite-sized books, co-written with Helge Fisher.

Overseas launches, book signings, a nationwide workshop programme, medical specialist seminars, TV and radio appearances, the launch of our own clothing range and magazine, sports workshops, fitness shows and conferences — all this has kept us out of mischief. But, immensely exciting as it all is, what really counts is the effect that Pilates is having on *you*.

We knew that Pilates worked. We were totally frustrated by the fact that the vast majority of the country had not had a chance to try Pilates and enjoy the benefits, and this, above all else, is what drives us. This is what it is all about and this is why we have decided to reproduce extracts from just some of the letters we receive daily.

Using Pilates I have discovered a strength and mobility in my back which I haven't had for years. When I first tried it, I was suffering from crippling back pain and spasms. Now I can't believe the difference. It's transformed my life and I 'sell' the method to anyone and everyone who even mentions back pain to me! I even completed the Glasgow half marathon last year.

Liz Doig, Helensburgh

It is by receiving such feedback that we really begin to appreciate the impact that the books and videos, and the Pilates Method itself, is having. This is sometimes underlined in the strangest of ways and none more so than when we were hosting a Pilates event one rainy evening at a central London book shop. A South African tourist who happened to be walking past the store on the way back to her hotel, recognized us and came in and interrupted us in mid-session – she had bought the book in South Africa, had been about to write to us to tell us how much it had helped her and to let us know that, quite separately, her daughter had recently called her to recommend that she buy the book (her daughter was following it as part of the prescribed reading for her fitness training course). This woman, on her first visit to London, couldn't believe the coincidence – it must be fate!

Our first book began by quoting Lao Tzu: 'The journey of a thousand miles begins with a single step . . .' Well, it's time to take you further on your journey, both in terms of your understanding of how and why Pilates works and, of course, with more advanced Exercises.

We have carefully graded all the exercises in this book. There are introductory exercises for those of you who have never tried Pilates before and to remind seasoned travellers in the Pilates Way of the basics of the Method. Then we have included intermediate and advanced exercises to challenge you and to enrich your workouts – to light the Way Forward . . .

Pilates . . . is designed to give you suppleness, natural grace, and skill that will be unmistakably reflected in the way you walk, in the way you play, and in the way you work.

Joseph Pilates

Introduction

A Success Story

Physical fitness is the first prerequisite of happiness.
Joseph Pilates

Something very exciting has been happening in the world of fitness. A revolution is occurring and, in the best tradition, it has its origins at 'grass roots' level. It hasn't come about because of aggressive advertising, attractive franchise schemes or pure media hype. It is happening because people are experiencing for themselves, through books such as this one and its predecessors, through videos and through the growing number of Pilates studios and classes, just how fantastic this method of exercise is.

Having jumped, pumped, sweated and strained their bodies through the seventies, eighties and most of the nineties, people are finally discovering an exercise technique which gives consistent results without the burn and the pain, and also without the risk of injury. Long-time devotees of Pilates learnt years ago to move with care, with direction, with thought and, as they now reach their later years, their lean, beautifully toned, strong, supple bodies are undeniable proof that the results last.

For most of its seventy-five years of existence, Pilates remained virtually exclusive to the privileged few, but it couldn't stay a secret for ever – and why should it? By its very nature, Pilates is probably the single most appropriate and effective exercise programme for the great majority of people. Physiotherapists, osteopaths and chiropractors, practitioners in both conventional and complementary medicine, impressed by the method's amazing success with back problems and spinal injuries, also noted its beneficial effect on the immune system, on osteoarthritis, on osteoporosis, on knee and shoulder injuries, on relieving stress and headaches . . . the list goes on. Now, Olympic athletes and international rugby and cricket stars have joined classes which were once the domain of ballet dancers and film stars.

What does it offer them? A dramatic improvement in performance and a sporting career much less prone to interruption through injuries.

Pilates enthusiasts have never had any doubts that the method worked, but what the medical profession has been able to tell us recently is precisely *why* it works and one of the things we will be doing in this book is to explain in some detail the technical side of the Pilates Method. It is fascinating and incredibly exciting that international research in the medical world has, in the last ten years, arrived at exactly the same conclusions as those formulated by Joseph Pilates in the 1920s!

But don't just take this on faith. You must try the method for yourself. Describing Pilates is somewhat like telling you what a particular food tastes like. Imagine for one moment that you have never tasted chocolate before . . . we could fill up several pages telling you just how wonderful its taste is. We could then tell you that it is made up of numerous ingredients and (usually too many) additives. We can talk you through how to make it, step by step. But after all this, will you really be any the wiser as to how it *really* tastes? Of course not. You have to try it for yourself. To experience it. And that is just what more and more people have been doing with Pilates which is why, in the United States of America, it was recently labelled 'the fastest growing fitness method in the world'.

Time to Change

Yes, you've heard it all before – just one more trendy fad in fitness, give it another year and it will all be forgotten! Not this time. The Pilates Method is here to stay because no other exercise regime changes you and your body the way that this technique does.

Pilates works on a completely different level. It actually changes the way in which you use your body. It changes the way that you move. By redressing imbalances and altering movement patterns, your body is brought back into balance. It will move the way nature intended – the way that you used to move as a child before you developed poor postural habits. This rediscovered freedom of movement will ensure that it is not only the muscular-skeletal system that functions efficiently but also the circulatory and lymphatic system. You'll not only look great from the outside but, right down to cell level, your body will become properly nourished with oxygen being replenished and toxic waste removed. With the Pilates Method's emphasis on mind–body integrity, what you are getting is a totally holistic fitness regime.

And there's more good news. You do not need expensive equipment, costly gym membership, or even hours of your valuable time to start to achieve results. The exercises in this book constitute a full body-conditioning programme, yet all you need are a few simple household items, an attentive mind, a little dedication and roughly three hours a week. Pilates matwork is about as minimalist as you can get, especially when compared with the heavy-duty machines and expensive gadgets most health and fitness clubs are set up with. The focus of our exercises is on you, not the machine or the surroundings. You are the star, not the equipment, not the music and certainly not the teacher!

This book is designed to be a self-help manual. One of the most important recent changes in the world of medicine is the recognition of the importance of self-help. It's time to change the burden of responsibility for our own good health from the expert, from the practitioner, to ourselves. Of course, you need specialist help and guidance when there is a problem or an illness, but there is so much that we can do to maintain our own health. It is your body, you only get one, and it's got to last you a long time!

Back to Basics

We have already said that Pilates works because it changes the way you use your body. If we are going to succeed, we have to take you right back to basics to unlearn all those bad habits and replace them with good ones to restore natural normal movement.

Let's look for a moment at how we move. When you want to pick up a pencil you don't have to think of all the different muscles needed to make that movement happen. After the decision to move has been made, our neuromuscular system chooses for us, selecting a combination of muscles to achieve the movement and sending instructions to the muscle fibres. It is a two-way communication channel, however, because the brain is also constantly receiving information back about where the muscle is, whether it's working, whether it's in pain, etc. This is our sensory feedback.

It takes a team effort for muscles to

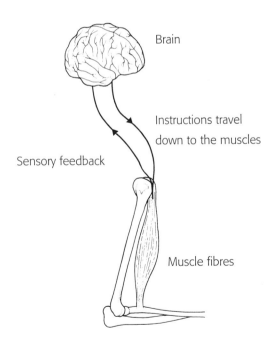

Brain

Instructions travel down to the muscles

Sensory feedback

Muscle fibres

Like a telephone line: the communication is two way

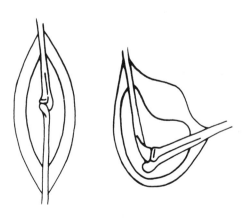

For a muscle to contract effectively, the opposing muscle must be able to lengthen and release

Muscle Fibres

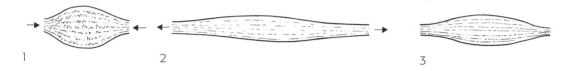

1. If a muscle is shorter than its ideal length it cannot function effectively
2. Longer than ideal length and it cannot function effectively
3. Muscles must be the right length and have the right type of fibres to work effectively

move bones as they usually work in groups. One may be the main mover while others add subtle direction or fix a bone in place, and opposing muscles have to release and pay out in order for the action to take place.

This group action is dependent on each member of that group fulfilling its role. But what happens when one of the muscles in that combination cannot work properly or perform as required?

Sometimes, for a host of reasons – such as poor posture, poor health, workplace conditions, sporting injuries, repetitive strain injuries – a muscle comes under stress. Muscle is a bit like elastic, in that if it becomes too short and tight, it cannot contract properly nor can it pay out or release to allow its opposing muscle to work. Alternatively, it may be too weak and stretched to contract effectively (see above).

Either way, the muscle concerned is out of order, and consequently the balance of the team is upset. Compare it to a football team. If one member is injured, he cannot play efficiently as part of the team. Similarly, if one team member hogs the ball, it

will also affect the way the team plays together as a group. The game must go on, so the team changes tactics to compensate.

With our bodies, the same applies. We still have to move, we still have our 'goal' – to pick up that pencil – so now we adopt a different combination of muscles to achieve the movement. This combination is far less effective, it is not what nature intended – not what the manager planned in his pre-match tactics – now you have a faulty movement pattern, a 'cheating' mechanism. Muscles have memories in that they remember actions and positions and, if these are repeated enough times, they become habits – in this case bad habits which, regrettably, can lead to pain.

It would be nice to think that taking up a sport or going to the gym will fix the problem. But what most of us do is simply take our bad habits, our faulty movement patterns, into the gym with us and reinforce the problem. In addition, many sports actually add to the problem by creating further muscle imbalance.

Take golf, for example. You don't have

to be a sports scientist to see that hitting a ball repetitively around the course is going to use the same muscles again and again. A typical club golfer will make virtually the same swing, using the same muscles, forty to fifty times per round whether from the tee, the fairway or the bunker – so you have the makings of a muscle imbalance in the body. No wonder so many golfers have back injuries. And that's just golf – you can apply exactly the same rationale to tennis, squash, football, rugby, swimming, athletics . . .

One of the explanations as to why Pilates works is because it rebalances the body, altering the way in which you recruit muscles to produce movement and changing the way you use your body, restoring natural, normal movement.

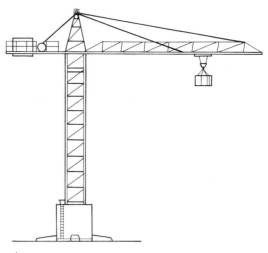

The crane

Balancing the Body

Let's take a closer look at muscle recruitment and these cheating movements.

We have already seen how muscles work together in groups to move our bones. They work as a team. In footballing terms, you have players with different roles – strikers and defenders. With muscles you have players with two roles – those with a mobilizing role and those with a stabilizing role.

Simply explained, the mobilizing muscles make big movements, such as moving the limbs around. In order to make these movements they work in phases, turning on and off. They tend to be more superficial, in other words lie closer to the surface,

and are usually quite long. They fatigue quickly and work at 40–100 per cent of their full efficiency or Maximum Voluntary Contraction. A good example are the hamstrings that run down the back of your thighs. They have several actions including flexing (bending) the knees and extending the hip (taking your leg behind you).

Now, while you are happily bending your knee or extending your hip, or even waving your arms around, other muscles in your trunk have to work to stop you from falling over, to *stabilize* you. You must have this stable base, in the same way that a tower crane needs a stable base while the long arm moves loads. These stabilizing muscles have to work for long periods of time, they need endurance. They usually lie deeper within the body, and are often shorter in length than the mobilizing muscles. They work at 20–30 per cent of their full efficiency (MVC).

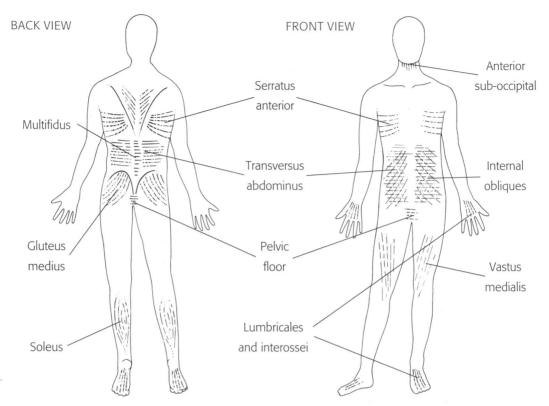

BACK VIEW   FRONT VIEW

Multifidus

Serratus
anterior

Anterior
sub-occipital

Transversus
abdominus

Internal
obliques

Gluteus
medius

Pelvic
floor

Vastus
medialis

Soleus

Lumbricales
and interossei

The main stabilizers targeted by Pilates exercises

When these two types of muscles work perfectly at their own jobs, the body is balanced, all the groups of muscles work in synergy and joints are held in their most favourable position, which is their natural 'neutral' position. You can see this in a person with perfect posture.

By studying the figure (right), you can see that all the joints in the body are held in their optimum natural position. When this person moves, with good muscle recruitment and the stabilizing muscles working correctly, there is going to be minimal wear and tear on their joints. The prospects for

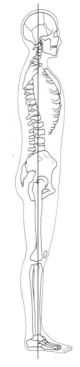

*Ideal plumbline
alignment
with skeleton*

his old age look good! Compare this, however, to the person below:

See how his upper body is held in a completely different way, probably through sitting at a desk all day. What has happened is that all the muscles around the front of his chest have been held tight and cramped. His head is poking forward and tilted back. His shoulders are held rounded, causing the muscles beneath the shoulder blades to be stretched. In terms of specific muscles, you can look at trapezius.

What is happening here is that the upper trapezius, which is primarily a mobilizing muscle, has taken on a stabilizing role. No wonder our neck and shoulders feel so tensed up. Meanwhile, the lower trapezius, which is supposed to act as a stabilizer of the shoulder blades, has been held lengthened and cannot work properly. There is a faulty movement pattern. The key to solving this common problem lies in

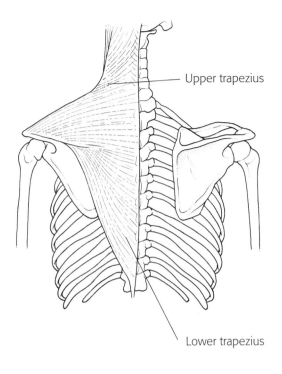

Upper trapezius

Lower trapezius

BACK VIEW

releasing tension from the upper trapezius and strengthening the lower trapezius.

Problems arise, therefore, when you have an imbalance in the muscles and therefore when the teamwork is upset. Back to our football team, if a defender cannot do his job for whatever reason, a striker may have to fall back and play in defence! When this happens to muscles, they stop functioning in the way they were designed to and start to take on different roles. When the stabilizers stop stabilizing, the mobilizers take on a stabilizing role. What you then end up with is the wrong muscles doing the wrong jobs, substituting and cheating to

Bad posture in the upper body

get movement. For the football team, they may or may not win the game but certainly their chances of winning are reduced.

What does this mean for us? It means that we are not using our bodies correctly or efficiently. If you are an athlete, you may never be able to achieve your full potential or your best performance and your career may be dogged by injuries. Non-sporting persons will probably develop bad posture, have body shape problems and may experience pain, back trouble, shoulder injuries, neck problems, tension headaches, knee injuries . . . We are totally unaware of the cause of the problem because the 'bad habits' feel familiar – that is, until the pain sets in. And until you tackle the way in which the muscles work together, you will not get rid of the imbalance. No amount of general 'undirected' exercise will help because the body will just continue to cheat.

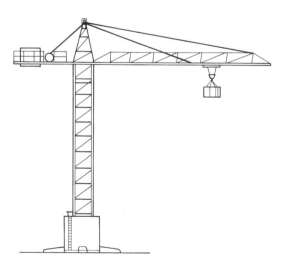

To lift a heavy weight or swing the crane – which part of the crane needs strengthening – the arm or the base?

Take Pat Cash, one of the most celebrated Wimbledon tennis champions of recent years. He did every type of fitness training. He looked, on the surface, to be extremely fit, but then he developed a serious back problem. Why, with all his fitness training, did he still have a problem, when we are told by everyone that exercise is the key to a healthy back? The answer lies in the way in which he was using his muscles. Put simply, his training combined with his heavy playing schedule developed his mobilizing muscles, but not his stabilizing muscles, which created a muscle imbalance in his body. This is a common problem with many fitness training programmes – they concentrate on the mobilizing muscles. Back to our tower crane image. If you want to lift a heavier weight than natural or swing the crane around – what part of the crane would you strengthen? The arm or the base?

Pat's story has a happy ending though. Following surgery for a herniated disc, which left him as 'stiff as a board' (his words), his physiotherapist recommended that he try Pilates. Precisely because Pilates works on strengthening the stabilizing muscles, those which lie close to and support the spine, the balance was restored and Pat was able to go on and play top level tennis once again.

How long does it take for this to happen? How many times does a movement pattern need to be repeated until it becomes automatic? You are talking thousands of repetitions – but who's counting? Suffice to say that it won't happen overnight, and that you are going to have to work at it!

Strength from Within

As small bricks are employed to build large buildings, so will the development of small muscles help develop large muscles.

Joseph Pilates

Just how did Joseph Pilates, with no medical training, way back at the beginning of this century, know about these stabilizing muscles? Their importance has only recently been discovered (see C.A. Richardson and G.A. Jull in *Manual Therapy*, University of Queensland, Australia). The simple answer is – he didn't! However, he had exceptional body awareness and he understood normal movement and how it could be restored. For example, he knew that when the navel was 'hollowed' back to his spine, he felt supported in his low back and similarly his clients didn't injure themselves. As a result, he therefore incorporated 'centring' as one of the method's basic principles. We now know that abdominal hollowing is the best way to engage the tranversus abdominis, the main stabilizer of the trunk.

Tranversus abdominis is the deepest lying of your abdominal muscles, it wraps itself around you like a corset. If you place your hands on your waist and cough, you can feel it engage. To obtain the very best stability for the lumbar spine we need to

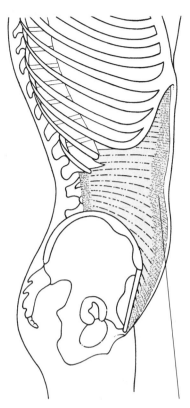

Transversus Abdominus
(your girdle of strength)

engage not only the tranversus abdominis but, also, one of the deep back muscles (multifidus) and the pelvic floor as well. This creates a solid cylinder which helps to prevent a vertebra shearing off its neighbour and out of alignment. This is the stable base of your crane. As these muscles are stabilizing postural muscles, they need endurance so we are looking at engaging them at about 30 per cent of what is known as their full efficiency or MVC. If you are asking yourself 'How on earth am I going to know when I've engaged them at 30 per

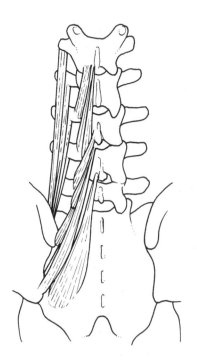

Multifidus. As you 'zip up and hollow' multifidus is engaged, stabilizing your lumbar spine

Feeling Good and Looking Good

The Pilates Method of body conditioning develops the body uniformly, corrects posture, restores vitality, invigorates the mind and elevates the spirit.

Joseph Pilates

Pilates is not just about stabilizing work and muscle recruitment patterns. It would be exceedingly dull if that were the case because, let's face it, remedial exercises are boring. The majority of people simply want to feel good and look good after a session.

Pilates is incredibly versatile and works on many levels. The 'feel-good factor' is not the least of them and it never ceases to amaze us how different clients look after they have finished a session. They often come in looking harassed, stressed out and positively grey and leave, after perhaps ninety minutes, looking as though they have had a two-week holiday (minus the sun tan).

An osteopath came in for a class recently. She was due to have surgery on a skiing injury and, therefore, had to work carefully to avoid aggravating the knee. At the end of the hour, she remarked that she felt '. . . lifted . . .'

After a recent knee injury, I found that my body had overcompensated and I felt completely out of balance. Pilates completely restored the balance of both my mind and my body and left me feeling elated and refreshed.

cent?', don't worry as we will be giving you very clear instructions to help get it right.

Of course, the lumbar spine is not the only part of the body which needs stabilizing. We've seen how the shoulder blades need to be stabilized or 'set' into the back, the pelvis also needs stabilizing, as do the knees, the feet, the neck, etc. Did Joseph Pilates know about these too? No. But he knew how to align the body correctly when exercising and he instinctively understood which muscles to work and how to isolate them. He had tremendous sensory feedback or proprioception. He knew how to encourage sound movement patterns. Seventy-five years on, he has been proved right.

There's nothing magical about it. The class had undoubtedly de-stressed her and hidden tensions had been released. The exercises had released those wonderful feel-good endorphins into the bloodstream. She felt 'balanced' not just in the muscle-recruitment meaning of the word, but mentally and emotionally. Meanwhile, behind the scenes, at a cell level there had been plenty of activity during the session, and her circulatory system and lymphatic system had been given a boost.

The heart and the blood vessels, together with the blood, form the cardio-vascular or circulatory system. The purpose of this system is to transport nutrients and oxygen to all body cells and remove their waste products. It is also responsible for transporting 'specialized cells' which fight infection.

The body is composed primarily of fluid and these fluids require constant circulation. It is largely the heart that maintains this circulation, driving the blood round the vascular system. You have about 100,000 kilometres of blood vessels inside you in the form of arteries, veins and capillaries. Blood returning from the body to the heart is low in oxygen until it has passed through the heart and pumped to the lungs where it is enriched again with oxygen. The oxygen-rich blood then passes back through the heart and is pumped back into the body.

The veins return the blood to the heart, and contain valves which stop gravity from causing the blood to flow backwards. The veins in the lower limbs have to overcome the forces of gravity for a considerable distance. Their valves often come under heavy stresses, resulting in a pooling of blood in the lower veins, with swelling and inflammation – varicose veins. It is the muscles contracting nearby, in the calf, which help the blood in the deep veins to move up. When you exercise the feet and legs, espe-

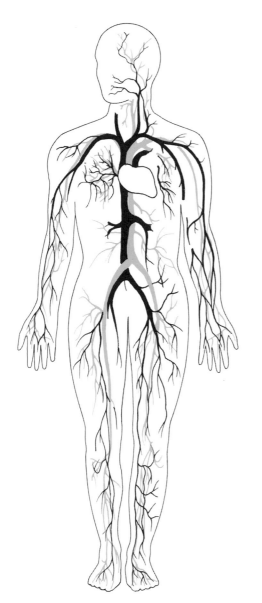

The circulatory system

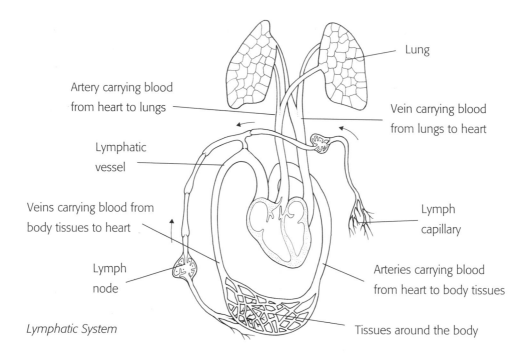

Artery carrying blood
from heart to lungs

Lung

Vein carrying blood
from lungs to heart

Lymphatic
vessel

Veins carrying blood from
body tissues to heart

Lymph
capillary

Lymph
node

Arteries carrying blood
from heart to body tissues

Lymphatic System

Tissues around the body

cially if they are elevated, the kneading effect of the muscles helps this venous return.

Similarly, the lymphatic drainage system, which has no heart of its own, depends to a large degree on the contraction and relaxation of the muscles during exercise to assist the lymph flow. The lymphatic network has enormous clinical significance as it helps to fight infection, filtering out disease causing micro-organisms. Unfortunately, it can become very sluggish. Fluid lost from the blood is constantly accumulating in the body's tissues. The lymphatic system is responsible for removing excess fluid from the body's tissues and returning it to the circulatory system. Interruption of lymph drainage in a particular area creates considerable swelling due to the accumula-

tion of fluids. Once again Pilates exercises can help

This is what we mean when we say that you are working on many levels with Pilates. You are not just changing the way you move; the movements themselves revitalize the body's own natural defences against illness.

As a heavy rainstorm freshens the water of a sluggish or stagnant stream and whips it into immediate action, so does the Pilates Method purify the bloodstream.

Joseph Pilates

This is one of the reasons why we have so much success with rehabilitation – restoring health to injured areas. Often these areas of the body become 'locked' and unable to move and, when this happens, they become blocked and congested. Nourishment fails to reach the cells and metabolic waste products are carried away inefficiently resulting in a toxic build-up which deprives them of oxygen. The body's natural healing processes cannot function and irritation, pain and sensitivity set in. It is very hard to break the cycle, especially when you are in pain and are afraid to move in case you make the pain worse.

Pilates exercises are so gentle and progressive that the cycle is broken. A session begins with the release of tension which is fundamental in the battle against stress. Body awareness is heightened to enable you to detect hidden tensions. The breathing alone can help enormously with relieving pain. The first movements are simple, not necessarily easy to do correctly, but certainly comfortable and within everyone's capabilities. As they are slow, controlled movements, you cannot cheat and they are quite safe. They are always performed in good postural alignment, so there is no danger of re-injuring yourself.

Once the basics of correct breathing, stabilizing and good alignment are taken on board, you can move on by adding more complex sequences which will bring together the Eight Principles of Pilates.

So we've discussed all the technical reasons why you should all be doing Pilates. If we haven't convinced you yet, we have one last card up our sleeve. Not only does Pilates rebalance your muscles, realign your posture, replenish and rejuvenate you, but it also reshapes you and makes you look fantastic. Why do you think so many Hollywood and theatrical celebrities are addicted to Pilates? Why do they visit their Pilates studios or call up their Pilates personal trainers when they have a bedroom scene coming up?

I was appearing in *The Beastly Beatitudes of Balthazar B*, a long, showy part, the climax of which was a striking appearance in Act Two, naked except for goggles and chains. I had two problems: a) stamina, and b) vanity. The latter was perennial; how to stop my passionate love of food from debauching my physique. The second problem was more practically pressing. Just getting through eight shows a week, during which I leapt from every corner of the set, was a real challenge. It was my theatrical agent who first mentioned Gordon Thomson to me. He took me and my body in hand. It literally changed day by day; there could be no mistake about it, because even the ushers in the theatre would comment, as I finally found my proper shape. There was no area of my life that didn't improve radically, from the study to the bedroom.

Simon Callow

No other method can change your shape so dramatically and so permanently.

Having said that, please don't make the mistake of putting Pilates into the 'hips and thighs' bracket. Although we may learn to isolate specific muscles we never look at them in isolation; the whole body is taken into account with every exercise. To concentrate on certain parts of the body for cosmetic reasons is quite simply asking for trouble, for the balance will be upset. The good news is that we do target the abdominals – it's our first step and, because we work them correctly, you can achieve the ultimate flat stomach without having to do hundreds of stomach crunches. Remember that with Pilates it is quality not quantity which counts. We want results which will last.

Similarly, if it's your ample buttocks and wobbly thighs that are worrying you, take heart as we work the gluteals and the thigh muscles as well. There are exercises for flabby arms too. Once you have absorbed the principles of Pilates, when you stand correctly with the spine lengthened and a strong centre, you will look one to two inches taller and a lot leaner. 'Long, lean and strong' is how health and beauty editors from the top magazines have described the typical Pilates body. As Jane Feinmann of *Family Circle* wrote: 'Pilates is a total joy . . . I felt taller, leaner and fitter.'

So not only do you move right, you feel good and you look great!

Joseph Pilates (1880–1967): A Brief History

Joseph H. Pilates, born in 1880 near Düsseldorf, Germany, suffered a childhood characterized by bouts of sickness, prompting him to take up physical fitness to improve his overall health and body image.

He moved to England before the outbreak of the First World War but soon found himself placed in internment because of his nationality. This was a catalyst for him and during this period he developed a very successful fitness programme for his fellow internees, many of these war veterans and amputees, as a means of improving their general health and fitness levels whilst being held in confinement.

After the war he returned to Germany and then moved to the United States where, in 1923, he established his first studio in New York with his wife Clara. The attractions of what quickly became known as 'The Pilates Method' coupled with Joseph Pilates' larger than life character, ensured that the studio became a favourite venue for dancers and performers, each working with an individual regime geared to their particular needs. Since those early years, many of the legendary names from Hollywood and the world of dance have benefited from working with the method – among them Martha Graham, George Balanchine, Gregory Peck, Katharine Hepburn, Terence Stamp, Joan Collins and Kristen Scott-Thomas.

The Pilates Method developed organically both before and after Joseph Pilates' death in 1967. Through his two books *Your Health* and *Return to Life* (the latter co-written with William J. Miller), Pilates introduced the world to a whole new approach to fitness and exercise. The exercises demonstrated in his books are highly specialized – beyond the reach of all but a few highly trained athletes and dancers – but they clearly show what can be achieved through Pilates or 'Body Contrology' as he often called it. New clients would be taught preliminary exercises and variations according to their particular needs. The fact that he never laid down a specific training programme means that those of his clients and staff who went on to teach the method each worked with a different emphasis based on their own experience with him. This explains why, today, virtually no two Pilates instructors teach in exactly the same way because they add their own personal expertise and experience to the key principles of the method.

More detailed background on Joseph Pilates can be found in *Body Control: The Pilates Way* by Lynne Robinson and Gordon Thomson.

The Eight Principles of the Pilates Method

During his lifetime, Joseph Pilates was constantly updating his programme, adapting the exercises according to his client's individual needs. This was his unique style. Since his death, the method has continued to evolve, absorbing the special gifts of talented teachers and also incorporating the latest research and advice from the world of medicine.

Our lifestyles now are very different from those of even forty years ago and, consequently, many of the physical problems we suffer are not the same. For example, we are far more desk-bound, many of us use computers which can bring about Re-petitive Strain Injuries (RSI), we drive everywhere and have labour saving devices. Stress is the new enemy. These factors have led to changes in the way we teach Pilates. The classical exercises have been adapted, simplified and new preparatory exercises introduced. In fact, were he alive today, Joseph may not instantly recognize the classes now taught under the umbrella of 'Pilates'.

This is especially true with the newer matwork routines, where many of the 'classical' exercises have been broken down into stages, making them accessible to a wider range of clientele. For many years, Pilates has been the preserve of 'professionals', dancers, performers, gymnasts, athletes, whose bodies were their living. Clients from all walks of life now learn the basics and build up step by step towards the classical matwork routines.

The exclusivity may have been lost, but quality has certainly not. Neither has the spirit of the method. The essence of Joseph Pilates' work, seen in the Eight Principles below, remains and underpins each and every movement. Pilates has simply evolved and finally come of age.

The Eight Principles are:
- Relaxation
- Concentration
- Alignment
- Breathing
- Centring
- Co-ordination
- Flowing Movements
- Stamina

The Relaxation Position

Relaxation

Taking time to relax and release unwanted tension from the body is the starting point in any Pilates programme. This doesn't mean that you should have a half hour 'nap' before the session – rather, that you should prepare both mind and body by letting go of the stresses of the day and by allowing any tension to melt away so that only the muscles you wish to use are used. Further, we have already discussed the importance of muscle balance and how the muscles work together to produce movement. It is very important that short tight muscles are lengthened before trying to strengthen the weak long ones.

For example, we all tend to hold our upper shoulders and neck tight, often wearing our shoulders as earrings. How can we possibly perform an exercise correctly with that tension still present? First release it, and then it will be possible to concentrate on the right movement patterns.

One of the best positions to help release tension is the Relaxation Position shown above (see page 32).

It is a good idea to spend a few minutes in this position at the start and the end of each session. However, it is not essential. You can omit this exercise and start with a gentle stretch such as the Studio Stretches (see page 34) as long as you focus on releasing tension from the body and the mind.

Concentration

The Pilates Method of body conditioning is gaining mastery of your mind over the complete control of your body.

Joseph Pilates

Pilates is at the forefront of mind–body exercise and, if you thought that mind–body was all about scented candles and dolphins singing, think again. Mind–body exercise should do just what it says: it should train both elements. How can we separate the two? Yet many fitness methods do just that! They focus only on the goal, the end product, and while you are pushing yourself to run that extra mile, do those extra repetitions, lift that heavier weight, you are not focused on *what* you are doing or on *how* you are using your body at that precise moment. You are so keen to reach the destination that you've missed the journey completely.

Pilates requires you to be constantly aware of how you are moving, it requires you to focus your mind on each and every movement that you make. It is mental as well as physical training, working on the neurological pathways from the mind to the muscles. It develops your body's sensory feedback, or kinaesthetic sense, so that you know where you are in space and what you are doing with every part of your body. Although the movements themselves may become automatic with time, you still have to concentrate because there is always a further level of awareness to reach, adding layer on layer. It could be described as a form of movement meditation, but without the spiritual overtones.

Alignment

If we are going to restore the muscle balance in the body to work as nature intended, then we must have the body in its right alignment while we exercise, otherwise the 'cheating mechanisms' set in. If we may return to our football team we discussed earlier, the players have to be in the right positions to play or there is chaos.

Different joint types

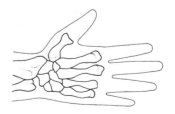

Saddle (CMC thumb)

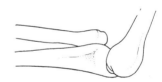

Hinge (humeroulnar)

Plane (intertarsal)

Condyloid (metacarpal phalangeal joint and knuckle)

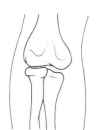

Pivot (superior radioulnar)

Ball and socket (hip)

Ellipsold (radiocarpal)

Good hip/knee alignment

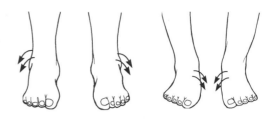

Rolling feet

By keeping good alignment, the muscles will hold joints in their 'neutral zone'. Joints are structures where two or more bones meet and articulate. While there are different types of joints (see page 17), we are most interested in synovial joints. These typically have two ends covered with cartilage and are freely movable.

Joint cartilage has no blood supply and depends on synovial fluid, which lubricates it, for its nutrition and health. Movement will flush fresh fluid over the cartilage bringing it nutrients. Without this lubrication, osteoarthritis may set in. For the cartilage to be healthy, it must be used regularly which is one of the reasons why exercise is such an important factor in keeping joints plump and juicy! If a joint isn't used then the cartilage isn't nourished and, in turn, it can become thin and even develop holes or ulcers. However, if the joint is held out of

its natural alignment and you exercise without due attention to its correct position, then the biomechanics of the joint are altered and there will be unwanted stress on them.

Take the knee joint, for example. If you bend your knee so that the kneecap goes directly over the second toe of your foot then you have kept the natural alignment of the leg and automatically maintained the balance of the muscles, working the deep stabilizers of the knee, especially the vastus medialis. If, on the other hand, you allow the kneecap to bend inward or outward, not only will the knee be under stress, but the muscle balance will be upset with a resulting knock-on effect potentially for the ankle and the foot, as well as the hip, the pelvis, the back, the shoulders, the neck and the head. If it is done repeatedly and becomes a habit, your body will try to compensate for the misalignment by perhaps altering the angle of your pelvis and then your shoulders and neck. The body will try to keep your eyeline level, so you end up having problems not only with your knee but with the rest of your body as well.

All parts affect each other. For example,

Allow your head to go
forward and up.

Allow your neck
to release.

Keep your shoulder blades
down into your back.

Keep your breast-
bone soft.

Keep your elbows open.

Lengthen up through
the spine.

Check your pelvis is
in neutral.

When you bend your
knees they should
bend directly over the
centre of your foot.

What about your feet
and legs? Usually they
should be hip-width
apart and in parallel.

Keep the weight even on
both feet – do not allow
them to roll in or out.

if you roll your feet in or out, it may affect your back. A quick check on this is to have a look at your shoes to see if they are particularly worn on one side. Clients are amazed when we give them foot exercises to help their neck, but no part of the body should be treated in isolation.

The right relationship between the head, the neck and the shoulders is also crucial. To engage the deep stabilizing muscles of the neck, you need to release the superficial neck muscles and engage the deeper, stabilizing muscles – the anterior sub-occipitals (see page 54). To do this you must relax the jaw and think of lengthening up through the top of your head, to keep the back of the neck long. We have already seen how the position of the shoulders will affect the muscle balance in the upper body. The shoulder blades need to be stabilized and set down into the back, using the lower trapezius.

Good alignment of each and every part of the body while exercising is crucial to safety and to correcting muscle imbalances. You have to be in the right position to get the right muscles working.

The correct alignment of your pelvis and spine is the starting point in Pilates. If you look at the shape of the spine, you will see that it is an 'S' shape with natural curves.

The Curves of the Spine

A man is as young as his spinal column.

Joseph Pilates

As we stand, the postural muscles of the body are working constantly to keep us upright. There exists a delicate balance between those at the front of the body and those at the back and any habitual change in the way we stand or sit will affect that balance. The spinal ligaments are affected in a similar way. If you repeatedly bend forwards or backwards, the ligaments will lengthen and the balance will be upset. Furthermore, the pressure within the spinal discs will increase. Even slight variations from neutral while you exercise can lead to problems. So, you must have your spine in its natural neutral position.

It is a similar story with the pelvis. A natural neutral position is needed to maintain the tissues at their normal length and ensure that the right muscles are used to produce movement. When performing Pillow Squeeze (page 42), if the pelvis is tilted or tucked as you curl up, the upper fibres of rectus abdominis and the hip flexors dominate and stability is lost.

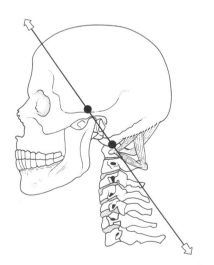

Head/neck relationship

Spine curves

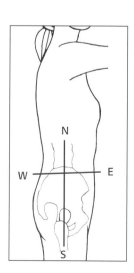

Correct

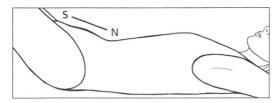

Tilted to North

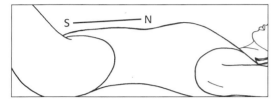

Tilted to South

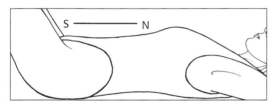

Neutral – the correct natural position of the pelvis

We recommend that you check your pelvic/spine angle constantly while you are doing the exercises. Meanwhile, the following routine will help you to find your natural, neutral pelvis and spine position.

Finding Neutral

Lie on your back with your knees bent and feet hip-width apart and in parallel.

Imagine that you have a compass on your lower abdomen, the navel is north, the pubic bone south, with west and east on either side.

We are going to look at two incorrect positions in order to find the correct one:

• Tilt your pelvis up toward north – while doing so, the pelvis will 'tuck under'. Notice what has happened to your waist, your hips and your tailbone (by tailbone we mean your coccyx bone, which is at the very base of your spine – at the crease of your buttocks, see spine on page 20). The waist is flattened because you've pushed it into the floor and the curve is lost. You have gripped the muscles around your hips and your tailbone has lifted off the floor.

• Now (avoid this bit if you have a back injury), carefully bring the pelvis so that it is tilting down towards south. What has happened? The low back is arched and feels vulnerable, your ribs have flared, you probably have two chins and your stomach is sticking out.

• We are aiming for a neutral position between the two extremes, neither to north nor south, neither tucked nor arched. Back with the image of the compass, the pointer is level like a spirit level. The tailbone remains down on the floor and lengthens away. The pelvis keeps its length and is not 'scrunched up' at all. There remains a small natural arch in your back. This is neutral, and all the exercises should be performed in this neutral position unless you are told otherwise. You would not start your car if the gears were not in neutral, so please do not start an exercise!

Be particularly vigilant when you are engaging the lower abdominals (see Centring, page 23) as then there is a temptation to tilt or tuck the pelvis. If you are lying down, you can always try placing your hand under your waist – you will be able to feel if you are pushing the spine into the floor. You want to avoid this.

It is also worth pointing out that if you have a large bottom, you will have more of a hollow in the lumbar region – this does not necessarily mean that you have arched your back. Learn to recognize your natural curve.

Bear in mind too that we also wish for the pelvis to be level west to east. Many people suffer from a twisted pelvis. The pelvis can be rotated forward on one side as well as tilted. You need to be constantly aware that the pelvis must stay neutral, level and stable while you exercise for the right muscles to work. Of course, there are exceptions such as Roll Downs (page 152).

Breathing

Above all learn how to breath correctly.

Joseph Pilates

In order for the body to receive enough oxygen to perform the exercises, we must breathe efficiently. Stand in front of a mirror and watch the way you breathe. Notice if your lower stomach expands when you breathe in, or do your collarbones or breastbone rise? Is there any movement in your back or in the lower part of your ribs?

Try to breathe deeply. Common habits include raising the shoulders towards the ears or, alternatively, allowing the stomach to protrude as you breathe in. The first is too shallow while the second is great for relaxation but impossible for Pilates, where we need to keep those lower abdominals back to the spine (see pages 23-27).

So how do we want you to breathe? Wide and full into your back and sides. This makes sound sense as our lungs are situated in the ribcage and therefore by expanding the lower ribcage, the volume of the cavity is increased and the capacity for oxygen intake is increased. It also encourages us to make maximum use of the lower part of our lungs. This type of breathing also works the muscles between the ribs, facilitating their expansion and making the upper body more fluid and mobile.

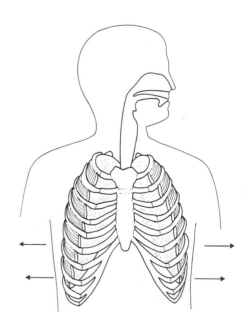

Lateral breathing pattern – breathing into the lower ribcage

We call it thoracic or lateral breathing. Your lungs become like bellows, the lower ribcage expanding wide as you breathe in and closing down as you breathe out. We do not wish to block the descent of the diaphragm on the inhalation but, rather, encourage the movement to be widthways and into the back.

Scarf breathing

To practice, try the following:

• Sit or stand and wrap a scarf or towel around your ribs, crossing it over at the front.

• Hold the opposite ends of the scarf and gently pull it tight, breathe in and allow your ribs to expand the towel. As you breathe out, you may gently squeeze the towel to help you fully empty your lungs, relax the ribcage and allow the breastbone to soften. Watch that you do not lift the breastbone too high. Be careful not to over-breathe or you may become dizzy – just breathe gently and naturally.

Not only is the type of breathing important to our way of exercising but so is the timing of the breath. You can help or hinder a movement by breathing in or out at the right time. All Pilates exercises are designed to reinforce and encourage carefully the correct muscle recruitment by using the breath.

Most people find this timing difficult at first, especially if you are used to other fitness regimes, but once you have mastered it, it makes sense. As a general rule, we:

• Breathe in to prepare for a movement.

• Breathe out, strong centre to spine, and move.

• Breathe in to recover.

Moving on the exhalation will enable you to relax into the stretch and prevent you from tensing. It also offers you greater core stability at the hardest part of the exercise and safeguards against you holding your breath which can unduly stress the heart and lead to serious complications.

Centring

We have already discussed at length the importance of stabilizing the trunk while we move. Clearly you need to have mastered engaging the deep stabilizing muscles before you begin the programme.

In order to achieve the best possible stability, you need to be able to engage the pelvic floor muscles at the same time as hollowing the lower abdominals to engage the tranversus abdominis.

'Pelvic floor, what pelvic floor?' you cry. We are talking about the muscles that form a sling underneath from your front passage around to your back passage. All your internal organs are resting on this sling.

It is equally as important for men as for women to learn how to engage these muscles. By strengthening them, both sexes can expect the following benefits:

• Better 'trunk stability' – these muscles act with the abdominal muscles to maintain intra-abdominal pressure during exertion, in that they also have a role to play in supporting the back.

• Fewer problems with incontinence and prolapses.

• Better sexual relations, including better orgasms.

• Fewer prostate problems for men and help in treatment.

It is not easy to isolate and engage the pelvic floor and it takes considerable concentration. The following may help you to find the right muscles:

• Try sitting with a rolled-up hand towel underneath you, between your legs.

• Make sure that you are sitting square with the weight even on both buttocks and then try drawing up the muscles of your front passage, as if stopping the flow of urine. Try not to tense your buttocks and never hold your breath while working the pelvic floor.

• Do not tilt your pelvis.

• Another useful tip is to suck your thumb while drawing up the pelvic floor. Sounds crazy and you feel daft . . . but it works!

The best stability is to be had when these muscles are engaged at the same time as the lower abdominals are hollowed back towards the spine. Whereas Joseph Pilates would have given the instruction 'navel to spine', we have recently introduced 'zip up and hollow' with great success. You need to imagine that you have an internal zip from

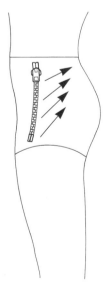

'Zip up and hollow' drawing up and in the muscles of the pelvic floor and hollowing the lower abdomen back towards the spine

your pubic bone up to your navel. As you breathe out, draw up the muscles of the pelvic floor and hollow the lower abdominals back to the spine as if you are doing up this internal zip!

The following three positions will help to ensure that no cheating goes on:

- Lie on your back in the Relaxation Position
- Check that your pelvis is in neutral.
- Breathe in to prepare and lengthen through the top of your head.
- Breathe out and draw up the muscles of the pelvic floor and scoop the lower abdominals back towards the spine, hollowing out your lower stomach. 'Zip up and hollow.'
- *Do not allow the pelvis to tuck under.* Do not push into the spine. Keep your tailbone on the floor and lengthening away.
- Breathe in and relax.

You must be careful not to tuck the pelvis under, that is tilting to north. If you do, you will lose your neutral position (see page 20) and it means that other muscles – the rectus abdominis and the hip flexors – are cheating and doing the work instead of the tranversus and internal obliques. If you are comfortable with your hand under your waist, you can check to see that you are not pushing into the spine.

You will notice that we have chosen to use the word 'hollow' to describe the action. It is very important that you do not grip your abdominals tightly for this will only create unnecessary tension and you will

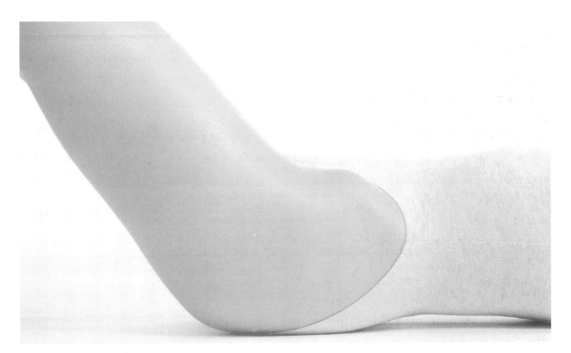

Navel to Spine in Relaxation Pose

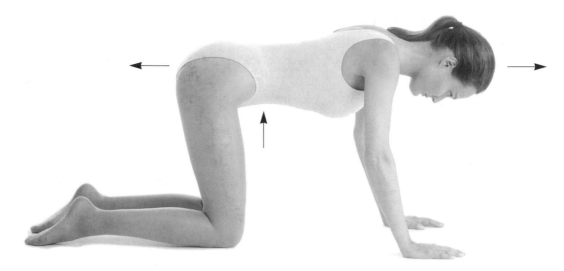

On All Fours

probably engage the wrong muscles to boot. Remember we said that we want to contract the muscles at 30 per cent. Think of:

- Hollowing.
- Scooping.
- Drawing back the abdominals towards the spine.
- Sucking in.

Have you found the right muscles yet? Another way to find them is on all fours:

- Kneel on all fours with your hands beneath your shoulders and shoulder-width apart.

- Your knees are beneath your hips. Have the top of your head lengthening away from your tailbone. Your pelvis is in neutral.
- Breathe in to prepare.
- Breathe out, zip up and hollow the lower abdominals up towards the spine. Your back should not move.
- Breathe in and release.

Still having trouble finding them?

- Lie on your front.
- Rest your head on your folded hands, opening the shoulders out and relaxing the upper back – you may need a small, flat

Precious Egg

cushion under your abdomen if your low back is uncomfortable.

- Your legs are shoulder-width apart and relaxed.
- Breathe in to prepare.
- Breathe out, zip up from the pelvic floor and lift the lower abdominals off the floor. Imagine there is a precious egg under them that must not be crushed.
- Do not tighten the buttocks.
- Breathe in and release.
- Again there should be no movement in the pelvis or spine.

This, then, is your strong centre and for most of the exercises, you will be asked to zip up and hollow, in other words draw the navel back to the spine before and while you move, your movements lengthening away from a strong centre.

One of the hardest things to learn in Pilates is how to keep the centre strong while you breathe in as well as out. This is crucial while attempting an exercise like the Double Leg Stretch (see page 72) or you will lose your core stability. To do this you need to be able to breathe laterally:

- Breathe in to prepare. Lengthen up through the top of your head.
- Breathe out, draw up the pelvic floor and hollow the lower abdominals back towards the spine, zip up and hollow.
- Hold this strong centre while you breathe into your sides allowing your ribcage to expand fully, keeping the stomach hollowed out and firm.
- Continue to breathe in and out, maintaining the strong centre.

Co-ordination

Concentrate on the correct movements each time you exercise, lest you do them improperly and thus lose all the vital benefits of their value.

Joseph Pilates

Now that you have mastered the breathing, the correct alignment, the creation of a strong centre and how to isolate the stabilizing muscles, we need to learn how to add movement co-ordinating all this. It isn't easy to begin with but, like learning to ride a bicycle, it soon becomes automatic. Meanwhile, the process of learning this co-ordination is fabulous mental/physical training because it stimulates the two way communication between the brain and the muscles. This is a real mind–body exercise.

We usually start with small movements and then build up to more complicated combinations. By repeating 'sound' movements thoughtfully and precisely, normal movement is restored.

Adding Movements

- Adopt the Relaxation Position. Check that your pelvis is in neutral, tailbone down and lengthening away.
- Breathe in to prepare.
- Breathe out, zip up and hollow the lower abdominals, and slide one leg away along the floor, keeping the lower abdominals engaged and the pelvis still, stable, and in neutral.

Leg slid away

• Breathe into your lower ribcage while you return the leg to the bent position, trying to keep the stomach hollow. (If you cannot yet breathe in and maintain a strong centre, then take an extra breath and return the leg on the out breath.)

• Repeat five times with each leg.

You need to maintain a strong centre while your arms move as well, so:

• Still in the Relaxation Position, this time have your arms down by your sides.

• Breathe in wide into your lower ribcage to prepare.

• Breathe out, zip up and hollow and take one arm back to touch the floor behind you, if you can. Do not force the arm, keep it soft and open with the elbow bent. The shoulder blade stays down into your back. The ribs stay calm. Do not allow the back to arch at all.

• Breathe in as you return the arms to your side.

• Repeat with the other arm.

• Practice five on each arm.

Note: Not everyone can touch the floor behind them without arching the upper back. Do not strain. It is better to keep the back down than to force the arm.

Now we are going to co-ordinate the

Arm above head – keep the shoulder blades down

opposite arm and leg. This is a sequence you first learnt when beginning to crawl as a child! Between the ages of four to seven months a child begins to learn to cross pattern, co-ordinating opposite arm and leg movement. This stage of development aids communication between the right and left hemispheres of the brain. Hopefully, everyone reading this will have mastered crawling, but as a neurological exercise it is helpful even for adults to practise and some of you may discover it isn't quite as easy as it sounds!

Co-ordinating Arms and Legs

- Breathe in to prepare.
- Breathe out, zip up and hollow and slide the right leg away along the floor and take the left arm above you in a backstroke movement. Keep the pelvis completely neutral, stable and still and the stomach muscles engaged. Keep a sense of width and openness in the upper body and shoulders and try to keep the shoulder blades down into your back.
- Breathe in, still zipped and hollowed, and return the limbs to the starting position.
- Repeat five times alternating arms and legs.

These may not seem like difficult movements but to do them properly takes great concentration and skill. You are basically trying to retrain your muscle recruitment, so please do not be tempted to skip learning these basic skills as they are invaluable in mastering the more difficult exercises.

Flowing Movements

Pilates is all about natural movements performed correctly, gracefully and with control. You will not be required to twist into any awkward positions or to strain. Movements are generally slowly performed,

lengthening away from the strong centre. This gives you the opportunity to check your alignment and to focus on using the right muscles to do the job. You can also stop if you feel any discomfort, making Pilates one of the safest forms of exercise. Slow doesn't mean easy though, in fact it is harder to do an exercise slowly than quickly and it is also less easy to cheat!

Stamina

As you become more proficient at the exercises and your muscles begin to work the way nature intended, you will discover that your overall stamina improves dramatically. You will no longer be wasting energy holding on to unnecessary tension or moving inefficiently. Many people complain of tiredness after a day on their feet. This is because standing badly is tiring. By strengthening the deep postural stabilizing muscles, endurance is greatly improved. Think of a well-tuned car engine, it needs far less oil.

The only thing that Pilates doesn't offer is cardiovascular work. Having said that, some of the exercises such as The Hundred (see page 64) will increase the heart rate but, generally speaking, you will need to add some aerobic work into your fitness programme. Brisk walking, cycling and swimming are all excellent, but bear in mind that you must use your body well while doing them or you will undo all the good you have done in your Pilates session. What Pilates can do is make you fit for your chosen sport or activity and ensure that the right muscles do the work.

Before You Begin

• Be sure that you have no pressing unfinished business.

• Take the telephone off the hook, or put the answering machine on.

• You may prefer silence, otherwise put on some unobtrusive classical or new age music.

• All exercises should be done on a padded mat.

• Wear something warm and comfortable which allows free movement.

• Barefoot is best, socks otherwise.

• The best time to exercise is in the late afternoon or evening when your muscles are already warmed up as a result of the day's activity. Exercising in the morning is fine, but you will need to take longer to warm up thoroughly.

• You will need space to work in – you cannot keep stopping to move furniture. Some clear wall space will be needed if you are going to do the wall exercises.

• Items you may need include a chair, a small, flat but firm pillow for behind your head or perhaps a folded towel, a larger pillow, a long scarf and a tennis ball.

Please do not exercise if:

• You are feeling unwell.

• You have just eaten a heavy meal.

• You have been drinking alcohol.

• You are in pain from an injury — always consult your practitioner first, as rest may be needed before you exercise.

• You have taken pain killers, as it will mask any warning pains.

• You are undergoing medical treatment, or are taking drugs – again, you will need to consult your medical practitioner first.

And remember:

• It is always wise to consult your doctor before taking up a new exercise regime.

• Not all of the exercises are suitable for use during pregnancy.

• If you have a back problem you will need to consult with your medical practitioner. Many of the exercises are wonderful for back-related problems, but you should always take expert guidance.

How to Use This Book

You've read the introduction and the Eight Principles, so where do you start? It is very important that you have mastered:

• Lateral breathing (page 22).

• Finding the neutral position of your pelvis and spine (page 20).

• Engaging the deep stabilizing muscles (page 23).

Practise these until you feel that you have absorbed them and then you may proceed with the exercises themselves. All the exercises have been graded according to their level of difficulty – all levels, intermediate and advanced. Remember that Pilates is not competitive, so only progress to the next level when you are confident that you can perform the exercise safely and correctly.

As a starter try the following session:
• The Relaxation Position (page 32)
• The Studio Stretches (page 34)
• The Pillow Squeeze (page 42)
• Spine Curl with Pillow (page 44)
• Hip Rolls, with feet down on the floor (page 46)
• Stabilizing the Pelvis (page 50)
• Shoulder Drops with Twist (page 52)
• Neck Rolls and Chin Tucks (page 54)
• Curl Ups with a Towel (page 58)
• Standing (page 93)
• Shoulder Circles (page 94)
• The Dumb Waiter (page 98)
• Standing Side Reaches (page 96)
• The Diamond Press (page 82)
• Rest Position (page 90)
• Rolling Down (page 152)
• Arm Openings (page 156)
• Relaxation (page 158)

At the back of the book you will find a section entitled 'Working Out the Pilates Way'. Here, we have given you daily, thrice weekly and twice weekly workouts.

Warming Up

Pilates not only rebuilt my body, after a series of operations, safely and effectively, it also toned and elongated my muscles so that I lost inches and looked slimmer and fitter than ever before. It is the safest, most effective, tranquil, enjoyable and rewarding form of exercise I have ever found. Quite simply – it works miracles.

Tracey Childs (Actress)

EXERCISE 1

The Relaxation Position

Aim

To prepare the mind and the body for exercise – it can also be used after exercise to restore balance. To release unwanted tension from the body, allowing the torso to widen and the spine to lengthen.

A wonderful position to relax in. It actually allows the spine to lengthen as the discs absorb fluid and plump up! We use this position as a starting position for nearly all the lying-down exercises.

Here we have combined it with lateral breathing and centring so that your body is reminded of these basic principles before you begin.

Starting Position

▷ Lie on a mat with a small, firm, flat pillow under your head if this is more comfortable. The idea is for your neck to be parallel to the floor. Allow your neck to release.

▷ Place your feet in line with your hips. Some people are more comfortable with them placed a little wider, in line with your shoulders – this is fine.

▷ Keep your feet parallel.

▷ Keep your toes in the same line – you might initially need someone to check this for you.

Relaxation position

▷ Let your shoulders widen and the elbows open by placing your hands on your abdomen.

Action

▷ Allow your whole body to widen and lengthen.
▷ Notice any areas of tension and gently allow them to melt into the floor.
▷ Imagine that you have sand in your back pockets. Allow that sand to slowly trickle out of the pockets and into the floor.
▷ Release your thighs and soften the area around your hips.
▷ Release your neck.
▷ Check that your pelvis is in its natural neutral position (see page 20), neither tucked nor arched. Your pubic bone and your pelvic bones should be level.
▷ Take your hands and place them on your lower ribcage.
▷ With your next in-breath allow your ribs to expand wide and full so that you are breathing into your sides and into the floor.
▷ As you breathe out, allow the ribs to close down and the breastbone to soften.
▷ Repeat five times.
▷ Now take your awareness to your lower abdomen.
▷ Breathe in wide and full.
▷ As you breathe out, engage the muscles of your pelvic floor, drawing them up as you hollow your lower abdomen back towards your spine. Zip up and hollow.
▷ Take care that you do not move your spine or tilt your pelvis at all. Your tailbone stays down on the floor lengthening away. Do not grip around your hips.
▷ If you can, keep these muscles engaged as you breathe in laterally.
▷ Repeat five breaths, staying zipped up and hollowed.

You are now ready to start your session.

EXERCISE 2

The Studio Stretches (Static Stretching)

There are three gentle stretches in this series, called 'The Studio Stretches' because they are used to prepare for machine work in many Pilates studios. You need to be warm before you attempt them. If you feel particularly stiff or cold, march up and down on the spot for a few minutes before stretching.

The Opening Stretch (all levels)

Aim

To gently lengthen the spine (stretching the spinal extensors) and the inner thigh muscles (the short adductors). To release tension from the shoulders, learning good upper-body use and using the stabilizing muscles of the neck and shoulders. To prepare the body for exercise with lateral breathing.

Please take advice if you have a hip or knee injury.

Starting Position

▷　Sit with your knees bent and the soles of your feet together. Do not bring the feet too close to you.

▷　This is a gentle warm-up stretch so you should be comfortable.

▷　Make sure that you are sitting on your 'sitting bones' (ischia).

▷　Your pelvis should be square.

▷　If you wish, you may sit with your buttocks against a wall to check that you are aligned correctly.

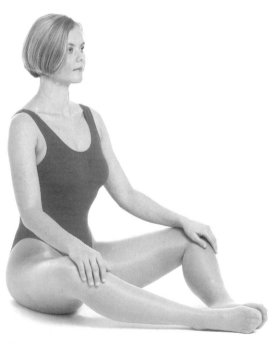

Start position (sometimes known as the Frog position)

Final position

Action

1 Breathe in to prepare, and lengthen up through the spine.

2 Breathe out, zip up the pelvic floor and hollow navel to spine. Lift up out of your hips and relax your body forward.

3 You are going to take twelve breaths in this position, relaxing into the stretch, reaching forward, but maintaining the strong centre. Breathe into your lower ribcage and back.

4 Your arms are resting in front of you, your neck is long, the top of your head lengthening away, your shoulder blades are resting down into your back.

5 After twelve breaths, on an out-breath, still zipping up and hollowing, slowly unfurl, rebuilding the spine vertebra by vertebra.

Watchpoints

▷ Breathe gently and rhythmically, feeling your back expand.

▷ Keep zipping up and hollowing.

▷ Do not overreach – you will get to a point where you may not be able to go down further.

▷ Check that the back of the neck, especially at the base of the skull, stays lengthened. Many people have a tendency to tip their head back.

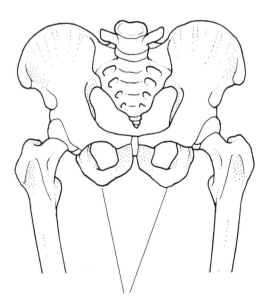

The ischia (sitting bones)

The Pelvis

The Hamstring Stretch (all levels)

Aim

To gently lengthen the spine and the hamstring muscles. To relax and breathe laterally. To become aware of the correct positioning of your neck, shoulders and pelvis. To use the deep stabilizing muscles of the neck and shoulders. To help focus your mind on your body.

The hamstrings are primarily mobilizing muscles which have a tendency to take on the stabilizing role when the body is out of alignment and has no core stability. As a result, they can become very tight. If you have in the past found that, in spite of continual stretching, they still will not lengthen, then you need the muscles to be balanced. You need Pilates!

Please take advice if you have a hip or knee injury.

Starting Position

▷ After completing the first studio stretch, straighten one leg out in front of you.

▷ Your pelvis must stay square – use the wall to help align yourself if necessary.

▷ Make sure that you are sitting on your sitting bones.

▷ Your straight leg is in a line with your hip and in parallel with it. The sole of your bent leg is resting on the inside of your knee. Your foot is relaxed.

▷ If you find it easier, you may like to sit on a rolled up towel.

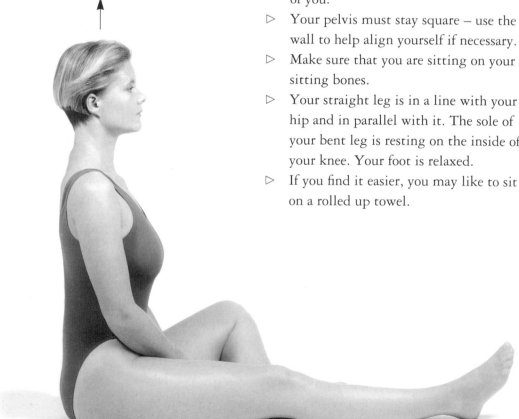

Starting position

Full position

Action

1 Breathe in to prepare and lengthen up through the spine.

2 Breathe out, zip up and hollow, and lift up out of your hips, gently stretching forward. Do not twist over one leg, but stay in the centre.

3 Take twelve breaths in this position, relaxing into the stretch. Breathe wide and full into the lower ribcage and back. Your neck is long, your shoulder blades down into your back and your arms are resting in front of you. Keep your weight even on both sitting bones.

4 After twelve breaths, breathe out, zip up and hollow, and slowly rebuild the spine vertebra by vertebra.

5 Repeat on the other side.

Watchpoints

▷ Keep the top of your head lengthening away, your jaw relaxed and your chin gently tucked in.

▷ Keep the weight even on both sitting bones.

▷ Do not lock the knee back, the straight leg stays straight but relaxed.

▷ Keep the foot relaxed.

The Final Stretch (intermediate level)

Aim

As for the previous stretches.

Please note: this is a more advanced stretch, so do take advice if you have back problems.

Starting Position

▷ After completing the last stretch, bring both legs in front of you, in parallel. Make sure that you are sitting on your sit bones.

▷ The feet are soft.

▷ You may still sit on the rolled-up towel if you wish.

Starting position

Full position

Action

1 Breathe in to prepare and lengthen up through the spine.
2 Breathe out, zip up and hollow, and lift up out of your hips and relax forward.
3 Take twelve breaths, relaxing into the stretch and breathing wide and full into the lower ribcage. Your neck remains long, the top of your head lengthening away, the shoulder blades stay down into your back.

4 After twelve breaths, breathe out, zip up and hollow, and slowly rebuild the spine vertebra by vertebra.

Watchpoints

▷ Do not overreach.
▷ If you feel any tingling in your toes, come out of the stretch.

The Fifty Flips (all levels)

Aim

To warm up the lumbo-sacral joint. This is a fun way to loosen this area, which often gets locked and compressed when we sit for too long. An unusual action, it's a little like shaking your wrist. The base of your back will feel quite warm afterwards from the extra blood flow!

Please take advice if you have an injury to this area.

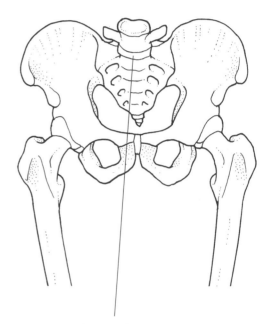

Lumbo-sacral joint

Starting position

Starting Position

▷ Lie on your back. Your head on a firm, flat cushion, if it feels more comfortable – the idea is to have your chin parallel to the floor.

▷ Your knees are bent, hip-width apart. The feet flat and in parallel.

▷ Your arms rest down by your side.

Action

1 Breathing normally, zipping up and hollowing, gently bounce your bottom rhythmically up and down.

2 Make sure that your bottom lands on the floor each time.

3 Aim to bounce fifty times!

Watchpoints

▷ Make sure that you 'land' each time you bounce.

▷ Keep the upper body relaxed.

As a veteran of many exercise fads and fashions, I have found in the Pilate's exercise method, the blueprint to maintaining a healthy body with neither the risk of injury or boredom in an environment free of stress.

Anne Summers

Full position

The Pillow Squeeze (all levels)

Aim

To isolate and work the pelvic floor in conjunction with the deep abdominals, engaging the deep stabilizers. To strengthen the inner thighs. To learn the correct position of the pelvis. To 'open' the low back.

This is a great exercise if you suffer from sciatica as it can help to release the sciatic nerve which often becomes compressed.

Equipment

A plump pillow.

Starting Position

▷ Lie on your back.
▷ You may use a firm, flat cushion under your head if you wish.
▷ Have your feet together, flat on the floor.
▷ Place a cushion between your knees.
▷ Check that your pelvis is in neutral.

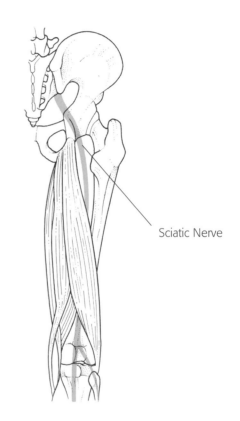

Sciatic Nerve

Action

1 Breathe in wide and full to prepare.
2 Breathe out and engage the muscles of your pelvic floor, drawing them up, and, simultaneously, draw the lower abdominals back towards the spine. Zip up and hollow.
3 Squeeze the cushion between your knees.

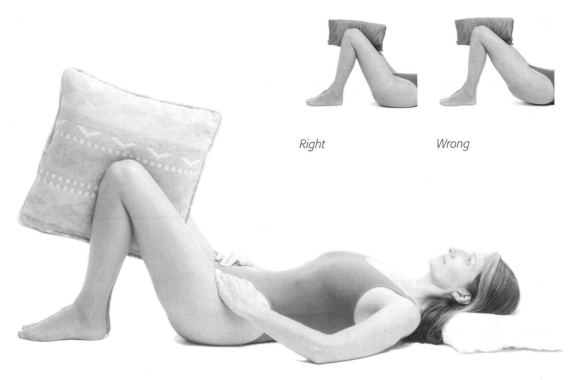

Right *Wrong*

Pillow squeezing

4 Keep the pelvis in neutral, the tailbone down on the floor, lengthening away. Try not to grip around the hips.

5 Continue to breathe normally, squeezing and working the pelvic floor and deep abdominals, for a count of up to ten. Then release.

6 Repeat five times.

Watchpoints

▷ Do not hold your breath – keep breathing.

▷ Keep your neck released and your jaw soft. You do not need to use your neck to work the pelvic floor!

▷ The most common mistake made doing this exercise is to lift the tailbone and tuck the pelvis. Think of keeping the length in the front of the pelvis, do not curl or shorten it. A good way to check if you are tilting is to place your hand under your waist. If you do the exercise wrong initially and tuck the pelvis you will feel the pressure on your hand because you are pushing into the spine. Now try to do the exercise with no pressure on the hand – you have stayed in neutral.

EXERCISE 5

Spine Curl with Pillow (all levels)

Aim

To learn how to wheel the spine, vertebra by vertebra, achieving synchronous segmental control, using the stabilizing muscles. To work the inner thigh muscles, the adductors!

The ability to 'wheel' the spine is an important aspect of your Pilates programme as many of us tend to become locked in one area of the spine (see pages 120–121).

Equipment

A plump pillow.

Starting Position

▷ Lie on your back with your feet flat on the floor and in parallel, up to 10 centimetres apart and about 30 centimetres from your buttocks.

▷ Place the pillow between your knees. Your arms are relaxed down by your side, with your palms down.

Starting position

Full position

Action

1 Breathe in to prepare.

2 Breathe out, zip up and hollow, and squeeze the cushion between the knees and curl the tailbone (coccyx) off the floor just a little.

3 Breathe in, and then breathe out, zip up and hollow, and slowly curl back down, lengthening out the spine.

4 Breathe out and zip up and hollow, peeling a little more of the spine off the floor.

5 Breathe in and then breathe out, as you place the spine back down, bone by bone.

6 Continue to curl more of the spine off the floor each time you go up on the exhalation. Inhale while you are raised and then exhale as you wheel the spine, vertebra by vertebra, back down on the floor. Aim to lengthen the spine as you wheel back down. The deep abdominals and pelvic floor stay engaged throughout and you keep squeezing the cushion.

7 Repeat five full curls.

Watchpoints

▷ You must not arch the back. Keep in your mind the image of a whippet that has just been scolded and has his tail (your tailbone) curled between his legs!

▷ Keep the weight even on both feet and try not to let them roll in or out.

▷ Keep your neck long and soft.

▷ There are some great variations to this exercise – try those on page 122.

Hip Rolls, with Shoulder Blade Setting (all levels)

We've given you two versions here. The second version requires very strong abdominals.

Aim

To stretch and work the waist, especially the oblique abdominals. To achieve a safe rotation of the spine, with segmental control (see pages 120–121). To promote awareness of the shoulder blades, using the stabilizing muscles (see page 23). To learn co-ordination skills.

What we look for here is rotation with stability. The ability to rotate the spine is the first movement we tend to lose as we grow old – well, only if we don't do Pilates!

There is a lot to think about with this exercise, which is great as we are trying to train the mind as well as the body! Focus on:

▷ Using the lower abdominals throughout.

▷ Peeling each part of your back off the floor in turn – first your buttocks leave the floor, then the hips, the waist and

Starting position

the back of the ribs. As you return to the centre, place each part back on the floor in reverse order – the ribs, the waist, the hips, the buttocks.

▷ As you turn the palm down, think of the shoulder blade setting itself down into your back.

Please take advice if you have a disc-related injury. If you have had whiplash, keep your head in the centre.

Starting Position

▷ Lie on your back with your feet in parallel and hip-width apart.
▷ Take your arms out to shoulder height, the palms facing upwards.

Action

1 Breathe in to prepare.
2 Breathe out, zip up and hollow.
3 Slowly and with control, roll your knees to the right, taking your head gently to the left, as you do so. At the same time, turn your left palm down, engaging the muscles under the shoulder blade so that the shoulder blade stays anchored to the floor.
4 Breathe in, still zipping and hollowing, and return the knees and head to the centre.
5 Turn the palm back up.
6 Repeat ten times to each side.

You may also like to do this with a tennis ball between the knees and the feet off the floor. See over.

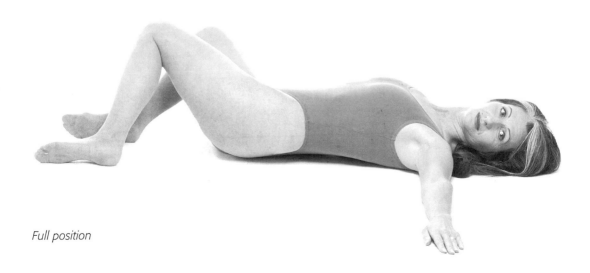

Full position

Hip Rolls with a Tennis Ball (intermediate)

Equipment

Tennis ball

Starting Position

▷ Lie on your back, arms out to the side, palms up.
▷ Your knees should be up towards your chest but in line with your hips. Your thighs will be at right angles to your body.
▷ Your feet are softly pointed.
▷ Place the tennis ball between your knees.

Action

1 Breathe in wide and full to prepare.
2 Then, as you breathe out, zip up and hollow and slowly lower your legs toward the floor
on your right side, turning your head

Starting position

to the left and your left palm down.

3 Keep the left shoulder down on the ground.

4 Keep the knees in line.

5 Breathe in and breathe out, bringing the navel to the spine. Use this strong centre to bring your legs back to the middle. The head returns to the middle, the palm turns up again.

6 Breathe in and then out, and repeat the movement to the opposite side.

7 Repeat ten times to each side.

Watchpoints (for both exercises)

▷ Keep the opposite shoulder firmly down on the floor.

▷ Hip Rolls with a Tennis Ball – keep the knees in line. Don't go too far unless you can control it.

▷ Use the abdominals at all times – feel as though you are moving the legs from the stomach.

▷ Do not force the neck the opposite way, allow it to roll comfortably and keep it long.

Full position

Stabilizing the Pelvis (all levels)

Aim

To learn how to stabilize the pelvis using the deep abdominals and the obliques. To learn to move the leg independently from the pelvis. To mobilize the hip joint, learning how to 'turn the leg out' and working the deep buttock muscles, especially gluteus medius, a pelvic stabilizer.

This is a super exercise for practising how to keep your pelvis still and stable (see page 23). You will find that your pelvis will want to tilt west/east to one side as your leg turns out – you have to prevent it. This is also a preparation for the Passé Développés leg weight exercises on page 146, as the initial movement is the same.

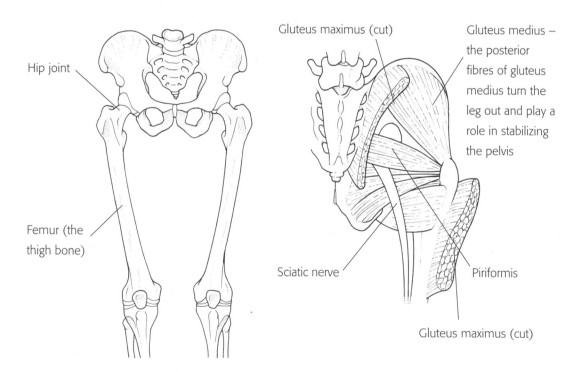

Hip joint

Femur (the thigh bone)

Gluteus maximus (cut)

Gluteus medius – the posterior fibres of gluteus medius turn the leg out and play a role in stabilizing the pelvis

Sciatic nerve

Piriformis

Gluteus maximus (cut)

Pelvis and thigh bone

The buttock muscles

Action 3

Action 6

Starting Position

▷ Lie in the Relaxation Position, using a firm, flat pillow under your head if you wish.

▷ Place your hands on your pelvis – this is to check if it moves.

▷ Find your neutral pelvis position.

Action

1 Breathe in to prepare.
2 Breathe out, zip up and hollow.
3 Fold the right knee up. Think of the thigh bone dropping down into the hip and anchoring there. Do not lose your neutral pelvis. The tailbone stays down.
4 Breathe in.
5 Breathe out, zip up and hollow.

6 Turn the right leg out from the hip, bringing the foot to touch the left knee, if you can. Do not allow the pelvis to tilt or twist, keep it central and stable.
7 Breathe in and then out. Zip and hollow as you reverse the movement to return the foot to the floor.
8 Repeat six times to each side.

Watchpoints

▷ You are trying to avoid even the slightest movement of the pelvis. Imagine a cup of tea, full to the brim, sitting on a saucer on your lower abdomen. The tea shouldn't spill into the saucer! If this image doesn't work for you, then try a very large gin and tonic in an unstable stem glass!

Shoulder Drops with Twist (all levels)

Aim

To release tension from the arms and shoulders, widening out the upper back. To stabilize the pelvis while rotating the upper body. To stretch the area between the shoulder blades and 'free' the upper body.

How many working days are lost each year through tension headaches? In searching for a cause for the headaches, we need to bear in mind that lack of flexibility in the upper body and rounded shoulders will contribute to the problem. Learning how to recognize tension and then how to let it go, is the focus of the next two exercises.

Starting Position

▷ Lie in the Relaxation Position with your knees bent and using a flat pillow

Starting position

behind your head if you wish. Your feet should be hip-width apart in parallel.

▷ Raise both arms directly above your shoulders with the palms facing inwards.

Action

1 Breathe in to prepare.
2 Breathe out, zip up and hollow.
3 Keeping the pelvis still and square, reach one hand up across the other to where the ceiling meets the wall. Your shoulder blade will leave the floor, your head will gently move with you.

Enjoy the stretch between the shoulder blades.

4 Breathe in and then breathe out and return the shoulder to the floor.
5 Repeat ten times to each side.

Watchpoints

▷ Maintain the gap between your ears and your shoulders.
▷ Do not overstretch, you should feel very comfortable with the movement.
▷ The pelvis must stay stable – do not allow it to roll with you. Use your lower abdominals.

Full position

Neck Rolls and Chin Tucks (all levels)

Aim

To release tension from the neck, freeing the cervical spine. To use the deep stabilizers of the neck (anterior sub-occipitals). To lengthen the neck extensors.

Forwards and up

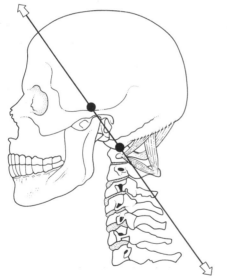

Back and down

An important aspect in re-educating the head/neck relationship lies in the relative strength of the neck extensors (those which tilt the head back) and flexors (those which tilt the head forward). If you think about how we sit at a desk or behind the steering wheel, we usually have our head thrust forward and tipped back – if you are short sighted, as we both are, you'll do this even more! As a result, you develop a muscle imbalance. We need to release the superficial neck flexors and engage the deep neck flexors. By relaxing the jaw, lengthening the back of the neck and gently tucking the chin in, we can redress the balance.

Please take note that we want you to *gently* tuck the chin in, nothing too vicious – it is a subtle movement. Imagine you are holding a ripe peach under your chin – you don't want to bruise it!

Starting Position

▷ Lie in the Relaxation Position, with your knees bent and your arms resting on your lower abdomen.

▷ Use a flat pillow for this if you are uncomfortable without one.

Action

1 Release your neck. Release your jaw and allow your tongue to widen at its base. Keep the back of your neck nicely lengthened. Soften your breastbone and allow the shoulder blades to widen and melt into the floor.

2 Now, allow your head to roll *slowly* to one side. Bring it back to the centre and over to the other side.

3 Just let the head roll slowly from side to side. Do not rush. Take your time.

4 When the neck feels free, bring your head to the centre and gently tuck your chin in, keeping the head on the floor and lengthening out the back of the neck.

5 Return your head to the centre.

6 Repeat the rolling to the side and chin tuck eight times.

Watchpoints

▷ Do not force your head or neck, just let it roll naturally.

▷ Do not lift your head off the floor when you tuck the chin in.

▷ If you find your jaw becomes tense as you tuck your chin in, gently place the tip of your tongue on the roof of your mouth, behind your front teeth, as you lengthen through the back of the neck.

▷ Try to roll your head directly to the side, rotating it around its central axis.

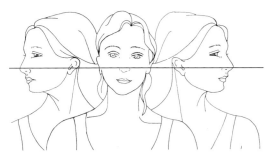

Girdle of Strength

Because of my rather stressful business life, I find that Pilates is just the antidote I need. The calm and concentrated atmosphere is so different from an aerobics class and helps me gather myself mentally and physically into a better, centred state. The Pilates technique is also perfect for what I am trying to accomplish with exercise: suppleness, lengthening, grace and control. In my interior design work, I try to create a feeling of sanctuary in the homes of my clients. Pilates is my exercise sanctuary.

Kelly Hoppen (Interior Designer)

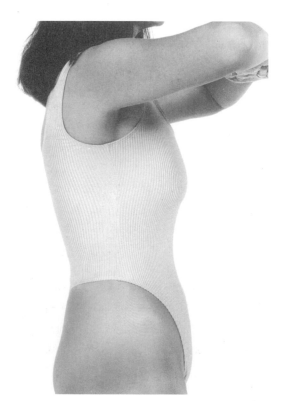

A quick flick through any magazine, men's or women's, will confirm that both sexes are obsessed with achieving a flat stomach. A typical letter from a member of the public to one of the fitness magazines will read as follows: 'I go to the gym regularly, do two step classes a week, and perform fifty sit-ups a day, but still my stomach sticks out. What am I doing wrong?'

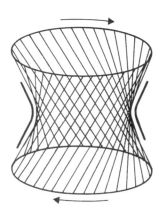

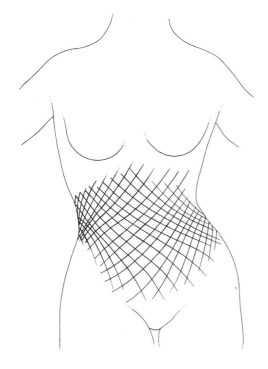

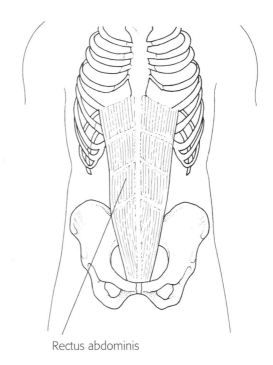

Rectus abdominis

We are aiming to create our own girdle of strength by strengthening transversus abdominus and the internal obliques

Most fitness techniques focus on strengthening rectus abdominus (the 6 pack). This is a superficial muscle which does not have a primary stabilizing role and it can often become over dominant

Our answer would be that the chances are that the correspondent is not doing the sit-ups correctly and, as a result, is actually adding to the muscle imbalance in their body, thereby making the flat stomach even more elusive. We are back now to the 'cheating movements' — those faulty recruitment patterns we spoke about in the opening chapter. In order to isolate the deep abdominals and use the right muscles to attain your flat stomach you must have the pelvis and the spine properly positioned and you must have the right level of awareness to engage the correct muscles. This is centring and zipping up and hollowing.

And remember . . . it is 'quality, not quantity' of movement that counts. The careful instructions given with each of the following abdominal exercises will ensure that quality if followed correctly.

Curl Ups with a Towel (all levels)

Aim

To strengthen the abdominals effectively, without compromising the neck or losing stability. To work the deep neck flexors.

The beauty of using the towel is that it takes the strain off the neck. It also encourages you to curl the upper body correctly. The action is very similar to the expensive 'Ab Curlers' you see in gyms. It's considerably cheaper though!

Note: if you have a neck problem or osteoporosis, please consult your doctor before attempting this exercise.

Equipment

A medium-size towel

Starting Position

▷ Lie on your towel with the knees bent.
▷ Have your feet hip-width apart, in parallel.
▷ Before you start the exercise allow your head to roll gently from side to side which will release the neck.
▷ Take hold of the corner of the towel with both hands above your head.
▷ Check that your pelvis is in neutral.

Starting position

Action

1 Breathe in to prepare.
2 Breathe out and gently tuck your chin in a little, as if you are trying to hold a ripe peach beneath your chin. Zip up and hollow.
3 Soften your breastbone, then gently curl up, making sure that your lower abdominals stay hollow and the pelvis neutral.
4 Breathe in as you slowly uncurl.
5 Repeat ten times.

Watchpoints

When doing this exercise please concentrate on four things in particular:

▷ The lower abdominals must stay hollowed throughout. Do not let them pop up.

▷ The pelvis must stay in its neutral position. Do not tuck at all. The tailbone stays on the floor lengthening away and the front of the pelvis remains long. Try not to grip around the hips.

▷ Think of softening the neck and the breastbone as you curl up, so that you do not use your neck.

▷ Keep your jaw relaxed and your chin *gently* tucked in.

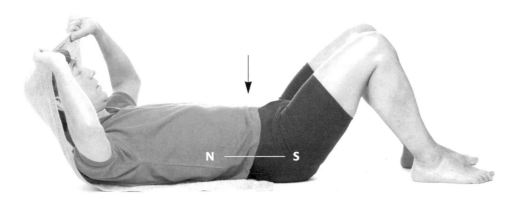

Full position – stay in neutral and keep hollowing

Oblique Curl Ups with a Towel (all levels)

Aim

As with the Curl Ups, we are aiming to work the abdominals correctly without strain on the neck but in this case, we are targeting the obliques.

Please take advice if you have a neck injury or osteoporosis – Knee Bends on page 62 is a good alternative for you as the neck remains on the floor throughout, but the abdominals are still used.

Equipment

A medium-sized towel.

Starting Position

▷ Lie on the towel with the knees bent, feet hip-width apart and parallel.
▷ Gently roll the head from side to side to release the neck.
▷ Check that the pelvis is in neutral.
▷ Take hold of the towel in both hands.

Action

1 Breathe in to prepare.
2 Breathe out, zip up and hollow, and

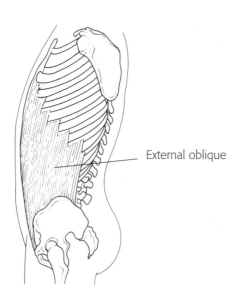

External oblique

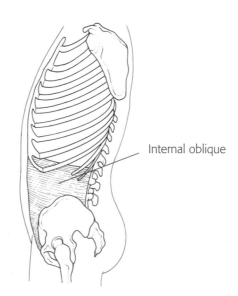

Internal oblique

Starting position

gently curl up, bringing your left shoulder across towards your right knee. Your stomach stays hollow, the pelvis square, your neck soft. Do not tuck the pelvis or allow it to roll.

3 Breathe in as you slowly uncurl.

4 Repeat five times to each side.

Watchpoints

▷ The lower abdominals must stay hollowed throughout. Do not let them pop up.

▷ The pelvis must stay in its neutral position. Do not tuck at all. The tailbone stays on the floor lengthening away while the front of the pelvis remains long. Try not to grip around the hips.

▷ Think of softening the neck and the breastbone as you curl up so that you do not use your neck.

▷ Keep your upper body open – don't let it close in.

▷ Remember also how in Shoulder Drops with Twist (page 52), you gently twisted the upper body while keeping the pelvis stable – the same applies here. Keep the pelvis square.

Full position

Knee Bends (intermediate level)

Aim

To strengthen the deep abdominals, maintaining pelvic stability without using the neck at all.

For many people with neck problems, even using the towel to help you curl up will place too much stress on the neck. This does not mean, however, that they cannot strengthen their abdominals. In this exercise, the head remains on the floor and it is the legs which move, which means we are still targeting the lower abdominals. It is by no means a soft option, as you will especially discover if you attempt the advanced version! For the exercise to be effective, however, you must have learnt how to maintain a neutral pelvis.

Starting Position

▷ Lie with your knees bent, feet hip-width apart and parallel. It is very important for this exercise that your neck is comfortable and relaxed throughout, so please use a firm flat cushion under your head if it helps.

▷ Check that your pelvis is in neutral.

Action

1 Breathe in wide and full to prepare.
2 Breathe out, zip up and hollow, and fold one knee up towards your chest.
3 Still breathing, zipping and hollowing, fold the other knee up.
4 Breathe in.
5 Breathe out, zipped and hollowed, and return the leg you have just bent up back to the floor and then, lastly, slowly return the other leg.

Starting position

6 Repeat ten times, alternating whichever leg you bring up first.

Watchpoints

▷ As you fold the knees up, think of the thigh bone dropping down into the hip socket.

▷ You must stay neutral. If you think you may be losing it – neutral that is – place your hand under your waist to feel the pressure there. As the knee folds up, you should not be pushing into the spine – you will feel some pressure, but it should be slight and should remain constant as the knee returns to the floor.

▷ Do not bend the knee too far up on to the chest. Study the photo carefully to help you gauge it.

▷ Those stomach muscles must stay hollow!

Advanced Knee Bends (advanced level)

This is far more challenging than it looks. You have been warned!

▷ Follow all the directions as above, only this time raise the legs just two inches off the floor, no more.

▷ Repeat ten times.

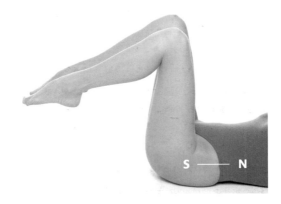

Watchpoints

▷ Keep the upper body relaxed and flat on the floor.

▷ Do not allow the head to be tipped back or the upper body to bow or arch. If this happens, return to the simpler version until you are stronger.

▷ If you feel either exercise in your back muscles, stop immediately.

Full position

The Hundred – Breathing (all levels)

Aim

To work the abdominals. To learn the breathing pattern of the Hundred, which involves lateral lower ribcage breathing to a set rhythm. To strengthen the pectoral muscles. To master stabilizing the shoulder blades.

The Hundred is a classical Pilates exercise – in fact, it used to be the warm-up exercise for mat classes. Well, it certainly warms you up! We have broken the exercise down into manageable bite-sized chunks. Try stage one first which is the preparation then, when you have mastered one stage, you may proceed to the next.

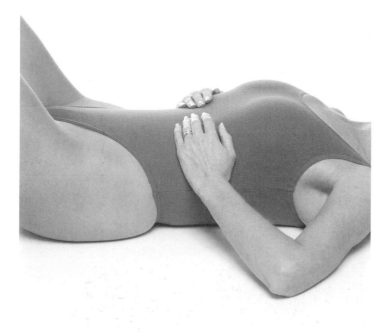

Stage one

Stage One

Preparation for the Hundred: Lie in the Relaxation position. Place your hands on your lower ribcage. Breathe in wide and full into your sides and back for a count of 5. Breathe out, zip and hollow to a count of 5. Repeat 10 times, trying to maintain the zip and hollow for the in and out breath. (If the count of 5 is too difficult – start with a count of 3 and work up.)

Starting Position – Stage Two

▷ Lie in the Relaxation Position. You may use a firm, flat cushion under your head, if you wish.

▷ Zipping and hollowing, bend your knees up on to your chest one at a time and in parallel.

▷ Your arms are extended alongside your body, palms down, wrists straight. Leave your head down on the floor.

Action – Stage Two

1 Breathing in wide into your sides and back, pump your arms up and down no more than six inches off the floor, for a count of 5. The shoulder blades stay down, with the fingers lengthening away. Stay zipped and hollowed throughout the exercise.

2 Breathe out and pump the arms for a count of 5.

3 Work up to twenty repetitions a total of one hundred beats – hence the name.

4 Slowly lower the feet one at a time to the floor – still zipped and hollowed.

Watchpoints

▷ Your breathing should be comfortable. Do not 'overbreathe'. If you feel light-headed, take a break.

▷ As you beat your arms be aware of any unnecessary tension in your neck. Keep the neck released, the upper body open.

▷ Your shoulder blades should stay 'down' into your back as your arms lengthen away.

Stage two

The Hundred Part 2 (intermediate level)

Aim

To continue with the breathing training, but now to add further abdominal training. To work the deep neck flexors while keeping the superficial neck muscles released.

Please take advice if you have neck, respiratory or heart problems. Avoid if you have osteoporosis.

Starting Position – Stage Three

▷ Lie in the Relaxation Position.
▷ Zipping and hollowing, bring your knees up on to your chest, one at a time, keeping the legs in parallel. Arms down by your side.
▷ Slowly roll your head from side to side to release your neck.

Starting position – Stage Three

Action

1 Breathe in wide and full to prepare.

2 Breathe out, zip up and hollow, and curl the upper body off the floor, remembering everything you learnt for Curl Ups (page 58). Chin tucked gently forward, relaxed jaw, soft breastbone, released neck.

3 Zipped and hollowed, start the breathing and the pumping action of the arms which you mastered in the last exercise. Breathe in laterally for five beats and out for five beats. Keep the shoulder blades down and a large gap between your ears and your shoulders.

4 Repeat twenty times until you reach one hundred, then slowly lower your head and knees one at a time.

Watchpoints

▷ Return to the floor if you feel any strain at all in your neck.

▷ To prevent strain and to engage the deep stabilizers, have your chin gently tucked in. Your line of focus should be between your thighs. The back of your neck remains long, the front relaxed.

▷ You must keep breathing wide into your lower ribcage or you will become breathless. If you do feel breathless, stop at once.

▷ Keep a sense of width in your upper body. Do not close the shoulders, keep the upper body open, the breastbone soft.

▷ Keep lengthening the fingers away.

▷ When this version becomes easy you may try straightening the legs into the air – but never allow them to fall away as your back will arch.

The Full Hundred (advanced level)

Aim

To learn how to stabilize the trunk and co-ordinate breathing, centring and limb movement. To strengthen the abdominals. To work the deep neck flexors. To stimulate the circulation. To improve stamina. To work the inner thighs (adductors) and deep buttock muscles, especially the stabilizer – gluteus medius – and the external hip rotators.

This version involves 'turning the leg out'. This is a familiar expression for dancers but we need to explain it for 'ordinary folk'!

To turn the leg out you need to think of rotating the whole leg outward from the hip joint, without moving the pelvis, as in Exercise 7 Stabilizing the Pelvis. The action takes place deep inside the hip itself as the top of the thigh turns out. Think of the head of your thigh bone being firm in the hip socket,

Starting position – Stage Four

well anchored there – this helps stability. You must take care that you do not twist the leg just from the knee joint as this can stress the knee. It is the entire leg which spirals out.

Note: this is an advanced exercise and should *only* be attempted when you are confident with the two exercises on pages 64 and 66 which are preparations for the Full Hundred.

Starting Position – Stage Four

▷ Lie with your knees bent up on to your chest, arms down by your side with your palms down.

▷ Allow your head to roll gently from side to side.

Action

1 Breathe in wide and full to prepare.
2 Breathe out, zip up and hollow, tuck the chin in slightly and curl the upper body off the floor, at the same time straightening the legs into the air in parallel – but now turn both legs out from the hips. Flex the feet, lengthening through the heels so that you feel the stretch on the inside of the legs but keep your legs anchored into the hips. Squeeze your inner thighs together and engage the pelvic floor.
3 Breathe in for five beats and out for five beats, pumping the arms as they reach towards your feet.
4 After one hundred beats, bend your knees and curl back down.

Sequence for Advanced 100 – Stage Four

Watchpoints

▷ The abdominals continue to work throughout – you should feel the inner thighs squeezing against each other and the pelvic floor engaging.

▷ Keep lengthening the fingers away from your ears. The shoulder blades stay down into your back.

▷ Keep the upper body wide and open, do not close your shoulders.

▷ Please come down immediately if you feel a strain in your neck.

The Double Leg Stretch (intermediate level)

Another classic! Once again we have broken this advanced exercise down so that you can progress safely and comfortably.

Aim

To strengthen the abdominals and the deep neck flexors. To co-ordinate the breathing with movement. To increase stamina. To strengthen the leg muscles.

Please take advice if you have any neck problems.

Starting Position

▷ Lie with your knees bent towards your chest.

▷ Clasp your hands lightly behind your head. Your elbows are open, in a line which passes just in front of your ears. You should be able to see them!

Starting position

Action

1 Breathe in to prepare.
2 Breathe out, zip up and hollow, and slowly curl the head up from the floor, breaking from the breastbone keeping the neck soft and long and the chin gently tucked in. As you do so, straighten your legs as much as is comfortable for you. The toes are softly pointed. Do not allow them to fall away from you. Keep your back anchored into the floor.
3 Breathe in.
4 Breathe out, still zipped and hollowed, and slowly lower your head to the floor, bending your knees on to your chest. Repeat 10 times.

Watchpoints

▷ Do not pull on the neck – the hands are only there to support the weight of your head.
▷ Keep a sense of openness in the upper body. Do not close the elbows or the shoulders.

Full position

Double Leg Stretch (advanced level)

Aim

To improve co-ordination skills. To strengthen the stabilizing muscles of the abdomen and the deep neck flexors. To increase stamina. To open the upper body and work the shoulders. To work the inner thighs and the deep muscles of the buttocks, especially gluteus medius and the external hip rotators.

This is the Pilates Method at its finest. A complex, choreographed sequence which effectively conditions the entire body, using mind–body skills. The right muscles are activated to achieve the movements; the stabilizers working as they should; the mobilizers working as they should. Free, graceful movements with stability. The instructions may seem lengthy, but this is because this exercise requires you to control every aspect of your body.

A word about the breathing . . . you will notice an unusual breathing pattern for this exercise. You inhale as you curl off the floor. Normally we breathe out as we curl up. Why? We tend to use the out-breath at the hardest part of an exercise, when we need most stability from the deep abdominals. The hardest part of this exercise is when the arms are taken back in a wide sweep, so that's when you breathe out.

Action 1 2 3

Let's take a separate look at the leg action – you are straightening the legs into the air in a turned-out position. In the Starting Position, the toes are touching and the heels are apart. As you straighten the legs, you move from toes to heels and then, when straight, you flex the feet.

Starting Position

▷ Lie with your knees bent, the knees 'open' from the hip. Your toes are just touching but your heels are apart.
▷ Have your hands resting on the outside of your knees. Your elbows are open, breastbone soft, shoulder blades down into your back.
▷ Gently roll your head from side to side to release the neck.

Starting position – Action 1

Advanced double leg stretch sequence

4

5

6

Action (Numbers correspond to the sequence on pages 74–75)

1   Breathe out, zip up and hollow. These core muscles should stay engaged now throughout the exercise.

2   Breathe in and slowly curl your upper body up from the floor. Gently tuck in the chin and, at the same time, straighten your legs so they are turned out from the hips. Flex the feet and lengthen up the inside of your legs to the heels.

Squeeze the inner thighs together.

3   Your fingers are lengthening away from you just below your knees on the outside of your thighs.

4   Breathe out, still zipped and hollowed, and take your arms up in a wide sweep to the level of your ears, not behind. Keep the natural curve of your arms.

5   Breathe in as you circle the arms back round to rest alongside the thighs.

6   Breathe out as you slowly lower your head back down on to the floor, bending the knees so that they are back in the Starting Position.
    Repeat ten times.

Action 2

Action 3. Feet flexed

Watchpoints

▷ Do not allow the abdominals to bulge at all during the exercise. Keep hollowing and keep lifting from the pelvic floor.

▷ Keep your neck long, and released.

▷ With the legs turned out and straight, make sure that you anchor the head of your thigh bones into the hips.

▷ Do not allow the legs to fall away from you – keep them up.

▷ Do not take your arms behind the level of your ears.

Action 4. Arms sweeping back

Action 5

Stabilizing the Shoulder Blades

Do you find your shoulders creeping up closer towards your ears with each day of the week? We all tend to hold tension in our shoulders. Sitting hunched over a desk all day, the muscles of the chest around the front of the shoulders (the pectoral muscles) become excessively tight. Add to this the way in which we poke our head forward and you have the muscles of the upper shoulders and neck – the upper trapezius, levator scapulae, anterior deltoids, the pectorals and the superficial neck muscles, in particular the sternocleidomastoid – all overworking.

We all tend to hunch over

While these muscles grow more tense, the muscles of the mid-back, especially the lower trapezius and serratus anterior, are held over-stretched and lengthened and the deep neck flexors, the anterior sub-occipital muscles, are weak. The shoulder blades themselves may be held in a winged position. Stand in front of the mirror and let your arms hang by your sides. How do they hang?

You can tell a lot about your posture from which way your palms are facing. The most common position is for them to face backwards because the muscles at the front of your chest are so tight they pull your arms so that they rotate inwards and the palms face back. The natural alignment is for the palms to face the body.

To correct this very common problem we have to change the way you use the muscles of the upper body and to strengthen the stabilizers of the shoulder blades, in particular the lower fibres of trapezius and serratus anterior, and, also, to release the tension in the upper fibres of trapezius. Similarly, we need to release the tense superficial neck muscles and strengthen the deep neck flexors.

But first, we need to open the chest and release tension from the neck and shoulders. Try:

BACK VIEW

SIDE VIEW

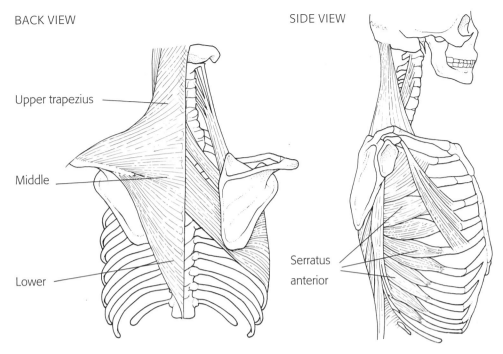

Upper trapezius

Middle

Lower

Serratus anterior

The muscles which affect the shoulder girdle

▷ Shoulder Drops (page 52)
▷ Neck Rolls (page 54)
▷ Arm Openings (page 156)
▷ Shoulder Circles (page 94)
▷ The Dumb Waiter (page 98).

With the chest opened and relaxed, we can then start to strengthen and stabilize the mid-back muscles which hold the shoulder blades down in the back, targeting in particular the lower trapezius. Try:

▷ Chicken Wings (page 80)
▷ The Diamond Press (page 82)
▷ The Dart (page 84)
　Also good are:
▷ Scapular Squeeze (page 100)
▷ The Albatross (page 140)
▷ The Dumb Waiter (page 98)

Remember, though, that we are trying to re-educate the body into good habits. So whenever you use your upper body or arms – for example with Scarf Breathing – keep your shoulder blades down into your back, your neck released and your elbows soft and open, lengthening up through the spine. By positioning the head correctly, lengthening up through the top of the head so that the neck remains lengthened, you automatically bring the deep neck stabilizers into play. The beauty of Pilates is that you are working the whole body correctly with each and every exercise. The following exercises target the shoulder blades and mid-back area, but as you can see from the lists of exercises above all Pilates exercises encourage sound upper-body mechanics.

Chicken Wings (all levels)

Aim

To develop scapular awareness. To strengthen the muscles which stabilize the scapular, especially lower trapezius.

For this exercise to be effective you must feel where your shoulder blades are and be aware of what they are doing. If you find the Starting Position difficult, try spending some time lying on your back with your arms out to your sides at shoulder height and with the palms up. When you are comfortable in this position you can proceed with the exercise.

Starting Position

▷ Lie on your back with your knees bent, hip-width apart, and pelvis in neutral. Use a firm, flat pillow under your head if necessary.

▷ Place your arms on the floor beside you. Put your hands on the floor, if you can, with palms facing upwards, fingers long. The elbows are bent in line with your shoulders (see photo), and the forearms should be parallel to your body.

Starting position

Action

1 Breathe in wide and full to prepare.
2 Breathe out, zip up and hollow, and slowly start to move your elbows downwards like chicken wings. You must engage the muscles below the shoulder blades to initiate the movement. You should feel as though the shoulder blades are connecting down into your waist.
3 The back of the hands will probably want to come up off the floor. You may rotate the hands inwards so that you are sliding them down on the edge of your thumbs.
4 Keep the arms on the floor and parallel to your body.

5 Keep your neck soft and long and have a sense of width and openness in the front of your body.
6 Breathe in, wide and full, keeping your upper body soft and open.
7 Breathe out and return the arms to the starting position.
8 Repeat 5 times.

Watchpoints

▷ Do not allow the upper back to arch up from the floor.
▷ Keep the pelvis in neutral
▷ Try not to use your neck at all, keep it released, and do not let your chin poke forward.

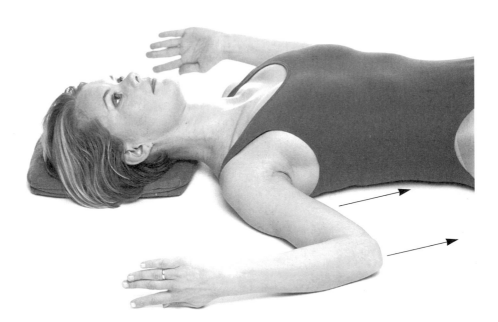

Full position

The Diamond Press (all levels)

A subtle exercise which has dramatic results. It really does help to reverse the effects of being hunched over all day. You can feel the tension in your neck release as the stabilizing muscles work. If you normally find extending your back (bending backwards) difficult, stick with this exercise for several months before you move on to the Dart.

Aim

To develop awareness of the scapulae moving on the ribcage. To work the muscles which stabilize the shoulder blades, especially lower trapezius. To work the deep neck flexors. To encourage lengthening while extending the back.

Starting Position

▷ Lie on your front with your feet hip-width apart and parallel.

▷ Create a diamond shape with your arms by placing your fingertips together just above your forehead. Your elbows are open and your shoulder blades relaxed.

Action

1 Breathe in and lengthen through the spine.

2 Breathe out, zip up and hollow, and pull the shoulder blades down into the back of your waist.

3 Lengthen through the top of your head and lift your head an inch or two off the floor. Stay looking down at the floor with the back of the neck long. Imagine a cord pulling you from the top of your head. Really make the connection down into the small of your back – you have to push a little on the

Starting position

Full position – side view

elbows, but think of them connecting
with your waist as well.

4   Breathe in and hold the position.
5   Keep the lower stomach lifted, but the
    ribs on the floor.
6   Breathe out, still zipped and hollowed,
    and slowly lower back down. Keep
    lengthening through the spine.
7   Repeat five times.

Watchpoints

▷ Keep the lower abdominals drawing
   back to the spine.
▷ Make sure that you keep looking down
   at the floor – if you lift your head back
   you will shorten the back of the neck.

Full position – from above

Incorrect Diamond Press – do not throw your head back

EXERCISE 20

The Dart (intermediate level)

Aim

To strengthen the back extensor muscles with trunk stability. To create awareness of the shoulder blades and to strengthen the muscles which stabilize them. To work the deep neck flexors.

Once you have learnt how to stabilize the spine and the shoulder blades, to breathe laterally and to maintain the length in your spine, we can move on to further strengthen the back muscles. For this exercise, imagine you are being shot out of a cannon!

Starting Position

▷   Lie on your front. You may place a flat pillow under your forehead to allow you to breathe.

▷   Your arms are down at your sides, your palms facing your body. Your neck is long. Your legs are together, in parallel with your toes pointing.

Action

1   Breathe in to prepare and lengthen through the spine and the top of the head.

2   Breathe out, zip up and hollow, and pull your shoulder blades down into your back, lifting your upper body off the floor and lengthening your fingers away from you down towards your feet. The top of your head stays lengthening away from you.

3   Keep looking straight down at the floor. Do not tip your head back.

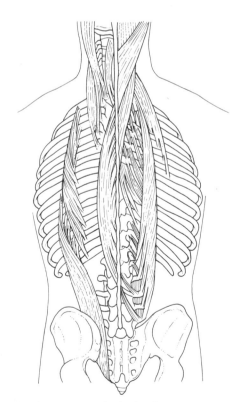

Erector spinae – extends the back

Starting position

4 Squeeze your inner thighs together but keep your feet on the floor.

5 Breathe in and feel the length of the body from the tips of toes to the top of your head.

6 Breathe out, still zipped up and hollowed, and slowly lower.

Watchpoints

▷ Keep hollowing the lower abdominals.

▷ Do not strain the neck, it should feel released as your shoulders engage

down into your back. Think of a swan's neck growing out between its wings.

▷ Please remember to keep your feet on the floor.

▷ Please stop immediately if you feel at all uncomfortable in the low back. It is possible to have the legs slightly apart, this is easier on the lumbar spine.

Full position

The Advanced Diamond Press (advanced level)

As the name suggests this is the advanced version of the last exercise. It should only be attempted when you have mastered the first version.

Aim

To work the back extensors, without strain on the back or the neck and maintaining the length in the spine.

Starting Position

▷ Lie on your front with your forehead resting on your folded hands.

▷ Legs together with the feet pointed.

Action

1 Breathe in to prepare and lengthen through the spine.

2 Breathe out, zip up and hollow, and lift your head and arms from the floor, sliding your shoulders down your back. Your feet stay together, pointed and on the floor.

3 Breathe in.

4 Breathe out, still zipped and hollowed, and lower back down, lengthening through the spine.

Watchpoints

▷ Do not come up too high or you will strain your back.

▷ Keep the sense of lengthening from the toes to the top of your head.

▷ Keep hollowing navel to spine.

Full position – shoulder blades down into your back – zipping up and hollowing, lengthening through the body

Like most of my contemporaries, my keep fit programme prior to discovering Pilates, involved disengaging my brain whilst performing mind-numbingly boring exertions on Stair Masters and other muscle-bulking machines.

Now, not only am I achieving the lean body shape that I truly desired, but for the first time in my life I look forward to exercising; finding the intense focus required of Pilates almost meditative and incredibly relaxing.

Lady Caroline Mactaggart

The Star (all levels)

Although not specifically aimed at stabilizing the shoulder blades, the next two exercises finish this sequence nicely.

Aim

To lengthen and strengthen the upper and lower back muscles, with trunk stability. To strengthen the gluteals.

Please note: if you are uncomfortable lying on your stomach, place a small, flat cushion under your abdomen to tilt the pelvis and start gently. If you have a history of sciatica, leave the legs in parallel.

Starting Position

▷   Lie on your front with your feet hip-width apart, turned out from the hips (but take note of the warning above).

▷   Take your arms out just wider than shoulder width so that you look like a star – remember to leave your shoulder blades set down in your back. You may like to place a small very flat pillow or folded towel under your forehead.

Action

1   Breathe in to prepare and lengthen through the spine.
2   Breathe out, zip up and hollow.
3   First lengthen then raise the opposite arm and leg *no more than two inches off the ground*, lengthening away from a strong centre. Do not twist in the pelvis. Both hip joints stay on the floor. Try to keep a sense of width in your upper body.
4   Breathe in and relax.

Full position from side

Lengthening away from a strong centre

Full position from above

5   Repeat with opposite side.

6   Repeat five times each side.

Watchpoints

▷   Do not overreach with the arms. Keep the elbows slightly bent and keep them wide.

▷   Think of creating space around the hip joint as you lengthen the leg away.

▷   Be careful to keep both hip joints on the floor – you are only lifting your leg.

▷   Don't let the pelvis roll or twist, keep it square.

▷   Keep your neck long and relaxed. The head stays down on the floor throughout the exercise.

▷   Everyone lifts their legs too high. You should aim to lift them only an inch or two.

Rest Position and Back-Breathing (all levels)

Aim

To lengthen and stretch out your sacral lumbar, middle and upper spine. To stretch your inner thighs (adductors). To learn to control your breathing in a relaxed position and to sense the filling and emptying of the lungs. To make maximum use of the lungs, taking the breath into the back.

Having just extended your back with the Diamond Press, the Dart and the Star, it feels wonderful to reverse the curve and come back into the Rest Position. You may like to experiment with pillows behind your knees, or under your head, so that you feel really comfortable.

Please note: if, for any reason, the transition back into this position gives you problems, when

you have finished the Star, roll on to your side and curl up in the foetal position.

Avoid the Rest Position if you have knee problems as you may compress the joint.

Action

1 Assuming that you have just completed the Star, come up on to all fours and bring your feet together, keeping your knees apart.
2 Slowly move back towards your buttocks.
3 Do not raise your head or hands and come back to sit on your feet – not between them – with the back rounded. Rest and relax into this position, leaving the arms extended to give you a maximum stretch. Feel the expansion of the back of your ribcage as you breathe deeply into it.
4 The further apart the knees are, the more of a stretch you will feel in your inner thighs.
5 With the knees apart further, you can really think of your chest sinking down into the floor.
6 You may also have the knees together which will stretch out the lumbar spine. **Please note**: we do not recommend this version for anyone with back injuries.
7 Take ten breaths in this position To come out of the Rest Position
8 As you breathe out, zip up and hollow, and slowly unfurl. Think of dropping your tailbone down and bringing your pubic bone forward. Rebuild your spine vertebra by vertebra until you are upright.

My job is physically demanding involving standing still for hours requiring strength and particularly steadiness in the upper body. Pilates has provided me with strong posture, muscles, strength and inner calm. I have only done without it for two weeks in ten years – it is the eau de vie.

Marjan Jahangari, Heart Surgeon

Stretching and Strengthening

I distinctly remember after only one session with Gordon walking out feeling a different shape, centred, grounded, and happy! As an opera singer it's given me a strength I never knew I had – but then came the challenge – what could it do for a body after triplets?! The books are the answer to my prayers – at home and at work!

Janis Kelly (Opera Singer)

The body will always sacrifice strength for flexibility and flexibility for strength. What we are aiming for are muscles which are both flexible and strong, and long and strong. Muscles that are overstretched will not work efficiently, neither will muscles that are overly strong. It is very unwise to stretch a muscle repeatedly without strengthening it and vice versa. Pilates gets the balance just right.

The following set of exercises are standing exercises which concentrate mainly on the upper body, strengthening the muscles which stabilize the shoulder blades and stretching tight muscles.

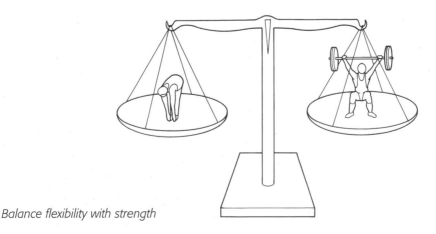

Balance flexibility with strength

Standing (all levels)

Aim

To find good postural alignment, allowing for good muscle balance throughout the body.

You may think we are being somewhat cheeky, calling Standing an 'exercise'. However, when you are trying to learn how to stand easily, it is difficult and requires great concentration and control. Later on, of course, it will become second nature.

Standing this way should be the starting position for all standing exercise.

Please read the directions from the feet upwards

Release your head upwards, towards the ceiling, while lengthening the spine. Imagine balloons on a string attached to the top of your head, lifting you up.

Let your arms hang comfortably by your sides.

Let your tailbone drop gently towards the floor as if you had a weight attached to it, but still maintaining the natural neutral spine/pelvis position (see page 20).

Gently release and unlock your knees.

Stand comfortably with your feet hip-width apart and your feet parallel.

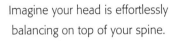

Imagine your head is effortlessly balancing on top of your spine.

Allow your shoulder blades to rest down into your back.

Keep a long waist.

Gently zip up and hollow, engaging the pelvic floor and hollowing out the lower abdominals.

Spread your feet on the floor, distributing the weight evenly. Imagine a triangle from the base of the big toe, the base of the little toe and the centre of the heel.

Shoulder Circles (all levels)

Aim

To release tension in the shoulder area, giving it a 'just massaged' feel. To be aware of the integration of the different shoulder 'parts'.

Did you know that the only place the shoulder

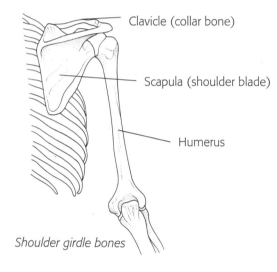

Clavicle (collar bone)

Scapula (shoulder blade)

Humerus

Shoulder girdle bones

girdle is attached to skeleton is by the collarbone (clavicle)? With the hip joint, the body has sacrificed some mobility for stability. At the shoulder joint, it's the other way around as the shoulder joint is very mobile but not so stable. At the capsule of the shoulder joint, stability is achieved by strong muscles and ligamentous tissue. It's no wonder that we are prone to shoulder problems when the delicate balance of these muscles is upset.

Lengthen upwards

Shoulders relaxed

Long waist

Strong centre

Soft knees

Weight evenly balanced

Starting Position

▷ Stand, taking on board all the instructions on the previous page.

▷ Stay zipped up and hollowed throughout the exercise.

Action

1 Imagine that you have a pencil attached to the ends of each shoulder or the top of the arm.

2 Breathing normally, rotate the shoulders backwards as if drawing circles with both pencils. Keep your neck released and the top of your head lengthening upwards.

3 Make the movement originate from deep within your centre from your breastbone and sternum.

4 Repeat five times in each direction.

5 Bend your elbows to give yourself chicken wings. Now, still breathing normally, circle the arms backwards, still working from within.

6 Repeat five times each way.

7 Hold your arms out now in a natural curve. The elbows are soft.

8 Circle backwards, moving the whole arm.

9 Repeat five times each way.

Watchpoints

▷ Be very vigilant about not tensing the neck or part of the shoulders (upper trapezius).

▷ Try not to poke your head forward.

Standing Side Reaches (all levels)

Aim

To stretch the sides of the waist, especially the quadratus lumborum. To achieve safe lateral movement of the spine with lengthening and stability.

This is a very common exercise. Unfortunately, it is also very common for it to be done incorrectly, with no stability, no alignment and no lengthening. It is a perfect example of how the subtleties of the Pilates Method make an enormous difference.

Remember to lengthen up before you bend to create space between the vertebra of the spine.

Please take advice if you have a disc-related injury.

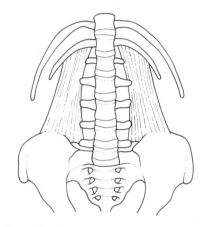

Quadratus lumborum

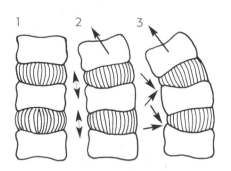

1. Vertebra. and discs
2. Lengthen up to keep the gap.
3. Without lengthening first you risk squashing the discs

Starting Position

▷ Stand with your feet wider than your hips. Have your knees slightly bent and remember all the directions for Standing (page 93).

▷ Your arms are down by your side resting on your thighs.

Action

1 Breathe in and lengthen up through the spine as you raise one arm up. Keep your shoulder blades down into

Watchpoints

▷ Be careful not just to bend sideways collapsing the waist – you must keep lengthening upwards.

▷ You must stay in line. Imagine that you are sliding between two walls.

▷ Keep the other arm on your leg, it will slide downwards as you bend.

▷ Watch the angle of your head. You want to keep the head on top of the spine, looking forwards. If you look down, you have lost that head/neck relationship.

▷ Keep your pelvis in neutral.

your back for as long as possible and keep your neck and upper shoulders soft. Finish with your palm facing inwards.

2 Breathe out, zip up and hollow, lengthening upwards as if you are going to reach towards the top corner of the room. Slide the other arm down the outside of the thigh. Feel the distance increase between your ribcage and your pelvis. Make sure you go directly to the side and not forward or back. Keep your focus ahead so that you do not look down or up.

3 Breathe in and keep lengthening upwards.

4 Breathe out, still zipped and hollowed, and slowly return to upright and then lower the arm.

5 Repeat five times to each side.

Feel the length in the waist

Full position

The Dumb Waiter (all levels)

Aim

To become aware of the shoulder blades and their relationship with the ribcage. To open the chest, especially the front of the upper arms and shoulders (anterior deltoids). To strengthen the muscles between the shoulder blades (rhomboids). All this to be done with the shoulder blades set down into the back, stabilized.

This exercise can be done anywhere, standing or sitting.

Starting Position

▷ You may sit on a chair or stand for this exercise. If you choose to sit, sit well forward on the chair with your pelvis in neutral and your feet planted on the floor hip-width apart, with your spread weight even on both buttocks! Hold your arms, with palms facing upwards, your elbows tucked into your waist.

Action

1 Breathe in to prepare and lengthen up through the spine.
2 Breathe out, zip up and hollow.

3 Breathe in and, still zipped and hollowed, and keeping your elbows still and into your sides, take your forearms to the side and backwards

Starting position

Full position

keeping them in parallel to the
floor, opening the chest and working
the muscles between the shoulder
blades. Keep the shoulder blades
down.

4 Breathe out and return the hands to
the Starting Position.

5 Repeat five times.

Watchpoints

▷ Do not allow the upper back to arch as
you take the arms back.

▷ If you find this very easy, check that
your elbows are staying in and your
shoulder blades are down.

▷ Keep your neck soft and released.

EXERCISE 28

Scapular Squeeze (all levels)

Aim

To strengthen the stabilizing muscles between and underneath the shoulder blades, opening the chest. To strengthen the back of upper arms. To lengthen the spine.

A wonderful exercise for the upper back and the upper arms, where unfortunately we all tend to get a bit flabby! Not any more, if you do this exercise and the arm weights series!

Take advice if you have back problems.

Starting Position

▷ Stand, feet in parallel, hip-width apart. Bend your knees, checking that they are directly over your feet.

▷ Now pivot forward on your hips as if you are skiing downhill. Your head, neck and back remain in one piece. Look at a spot on the floor in front of you at a distance that keeps the back of your neck free from tension and the top of the head lengthening away (see photo).

▷ Take your arms behind you to the sides with the palms facing upwards.

Starting position

Action

1 Breathe in to prepare and lengthen up through the spine.
2 Breathe out, zip up and hollow, and slide the shoulder blades down your back before you squeeze them together. Your arms are also squeezing towards each other as if the thumbs want to meet.
3 Breathe in and hold.
4 Breathe out and release the arms.
5 Repeat five times before returning to upright. When coming back to an upright position, stay zipped and hollowed. Keep lengthening your back and head away and return to a balanced way of standing without 'locking' your knees.

Watchpoints

▷ Keep your gaze on your spot on the floor.
▷ Check your neck, keep it released and long.
▷ Think of the tailbone lengthening downwards away from the top of your head.
▷ Keep the knees softly bent and over your feet.
▷ Make sure that you are feeling this exercise between the shoulder blades and also at the back of your upper arms. Do not lock the arms; they should be straight but not locked.

Full position – shoulder blades set down in the back and squeezed together

EXERCISE 29

The Up and Over (intermediate level)

Aim

To take the shoulder through its full range of motion, so opening the chest.

This is a difficult mobilizing exercise which should only be attempted when you have good mobility in your shoulders. You get a fantastic feeling of opening. It can be done with either a scarf or a pole. The scarf is slightly easier as it is more forgiving.

Equipment

A scarf or pole.

Starting Position

▷ Stand with the feet hip-width apart and thinking of all the directions given in Standing on page 93.

▷ Hold a scarf or a pole in front of you. Have your hands about one metre apart with the arms straight but not locked. Keep the elbows soft. Do not grip the pole or scarf too tightly.

Starting position

Second position

Watchpoints

▷ Do not be tempted to duck your head under the pole. If you have to do this, then you are not yet ready for this exercise.

▷ Do not lock the arms, nor bend one elbow. That's cheating!

▷ Take care that you do not arch the back as your arms come up and over. Keep lengthening through the top of your head, navel to spine.

Action

1 Breathe in and lengthen up through the spine.

2 Breathe out, zip up and hollow, and bring the scarf or pole slowly upwards, keeping the upper shoulders down and setting your shoulder blades down into your back. Now, if you can, take the scarf or pole right back in a large circle to touch your buttocks. The idea is not to bend either elbow to achieve this, the arms move in symmetry.

3 Breathe in and raise the pole overhead, breathe out as you circle the arms back over and in front of you.

4 Repeat five times.

Full position

Against the Wall

As a film producer with a fairly erratic life-style, I have always found a Pilates session a haven of sanity. This book is a wonderful introduction to a physically transforming system which is formidably effective in relieving tension. This book will be a godsend to take on location and will convert even those phobic about exercise.

Lynda Myles (Film Producer)

The Wall Stretches

These exercises look deceptively easy. We used to start all our Pilates classes in Australia with these exercises – clients would arrive late deliberately just to avoid them!

This first set requires you to have your legs up a wall. This position is fabulous for improving the circulation in your legs. With the legs elevated, the 'calf pump' works doubly well. As the muscles tighten and relax they help the veins to pump the blood back to the heart (venous return). If you suffer from varicose veins, where the valves in the veins have failed and blood is allowed to seep out into the surrounding tissue and there is a blockage in the system, these exercises will help to clear that blockage.

For the initial exercises you should have your buttocks as close to the wall as possible. If you have short hamstrings this will prove difficult so we suggest that you only come as close to the wall as is comfortable. You should feel your tailbone still in contact with the floor. Your pelvis is in neutral. Have a flat pillow behind your head if necessary. Unless directed otherwise, your breathing should be normal for these exercises.

There is no elegant way to get into this position. It is easiest to roll on to your side and shuffle your bottom up to the wall as close as you can and then swing your legs round and up the wall.

On a practical note, you would be wise not to use a wall covered with your best designer wallpaper, as you are likely to leave heel marks on it!

Please note: when you have finished the wall exercises, roll on to your side and rest for a few minutes before standing up.

The Basic Wall Stretch (all levels)

Aim

To lengthen the entire body, especially the spine. To relax and widen the upper body, especially the area around the shoulder blades. To improve the circulation in the legs.

Starting Position

▷ Get yourself into the position described above, remembering that your tailbone must stay in contact with the floor, so if your hamstrings

are tight, come back away from the wall and bend the knees. Either way your legs should be hip-width apart and in parallel. It is very important that you do not lose the neutral pelvis/spine position and that your upper back does not arch.

Action

1 Take your arms behind you, soft and wide and relax them on to the floor if you can. If not, leave them out to your side, palms up. Remember to keep your shoulder blades down into your back. Do not allow the upper back to arch. Your neck is released. Allow the spine to lengthen.

2 Work up to spending 2 minutes in this position, bearing in mind that if you are going to continue with the following exercises then you will be in this position for quite some time, so judge it carefully.

3 When you have finished, bend the knees gently and bring your arms down by your side.

Ankle Circles (all levels)

Aim

To mobilize and strengthen the ankle joints. To work the muscles of the lower leg. To improve circulation. To stretch the hamstrings.

Starting Position

▷ As for the previous exercise. Check that you are square to the wall and not at an angle.

▷ Your pelvis is in neutral.

▷ You may have your head on a flat pillow if necessary.

▷ Your legs are hip-width apart and in parallel!

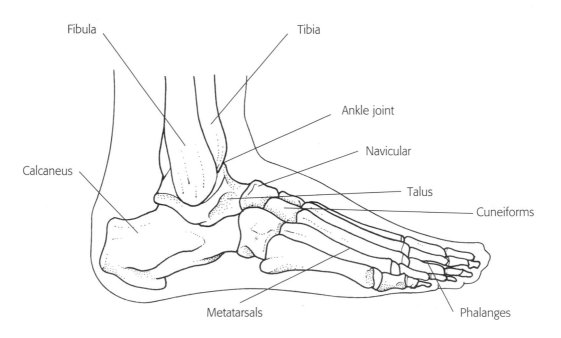

The ankle joint

Ankle Circles

Action

1 Keeping the legs completely still, rotate the feet outwards, circling from the ankle joints themselves. You should be circling very, very slowly and as far as you can.

2 Repeat ten circles in each direction

Watchpoints

▷ Don't just twiddle the toes around, work from the ankle joints.

▷ When we say keep the legs still, we mean still! And in parallel.

Point and Flex (all levels)

Aim

To work all the muscles of the foot and lower leg. To stretch the hamstrings. You'll feel this one in your shins!

Starting Position

▷   As for the previous exercise.

1 Starting position

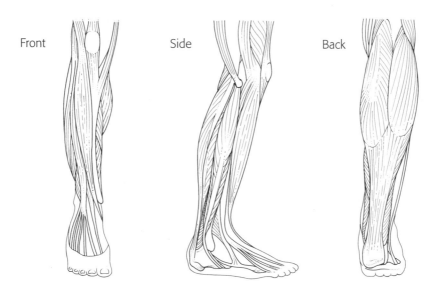

Front   Side   Back

The calf muscles

2

3

Action

1 Keep the legs in parallel, hip-width apart, and point your toes up towards the ceiling.
2 Now flex the toes only down towards your face.
3 Keeping the toes flexed, flex the feet down towards your face, lengthening through the heels.
4 Relax the toes.
5 Repeat ten times.

Watchpoints

▷ Make sure that your tailbone is still in contact with the floor.
▷ Bend your knees a little if the stretch in your hamstrings is too great.

EXERCISE 33

Creeping Toes (all levels)

Aim

To work the muscles of the feet.

Starting Position

▷   As for the previous exercise, but move
away from the wall a few inches. Bend
your knees so that your feet are flat on

the wall, still parallel and hip-width apart.

Action

1 You are going to spread your toes as wide as possible, then scrunch them up as if you are going to pick up a pencil with them. This action should bring your feet up the wall a little.

2 Carry on scrunching and creeping the feet up the wall until they cannot stay flat. Bend your knees so your feet are flat on the wall and start again.

3 Do five creeps.

Watchpoint

▷ Keep the legs in parallel, trying not to allow the knees to fall inwards or outwards.

Barre Exercises (all levels)

Aim

To strengthen the leg muscles, especially the quadriceps and, in particular, the vastus medialis. To learn correct alignment of the legs. To achieve pelvic stability.

These traditional barre exercises are a great workout for the legs and are proof that you do not need expensive or elaborate equipment to achieve results.

Alignment is everything for this exercise. By bending the knee correctly over the foot and keeping

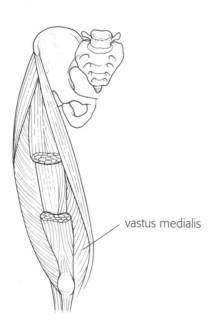

vastus medialis

The quadriceps at the front of your thigh

Starting position

the wall, still parallel and hip-width apart.

Action

1   You are going to spread your toes as wide as possible, then scrunch them up as if you are going to pick up a pencil with them. This action should bring your feet up the wall a little.

2   Carry on scrunching and creeping the feet up the wall until they cannot stay flat. Bend your knees so your feet are flat on the wall and start again.

3   Do five creeps.

Watchpoint

▷   Keep the legs in parallel, trying not to allow the knees to fall inwards or outwards.

Wide Leg Stretch (intermediate level)

Aim

To stretch the inner thighs (adductors). A deliciously uncomfortable stretch!

Please take advice if you have a knee injury.

Starting Position

▷ You'll need to shuffle back close to the wall again with your legs straight up. Only come as close as is comfortable. Use your head pillow if you wish. Check that you are square on to the wall.

▷ You may put your hands under your buttocks if it helps – you should certainly do this if you have back problems.

Action

1 Slowly widen your legs until you can feel a stretch on the inner thigh. Allow the legs to bend a little or roll outwards if they wish. The feet should remain level with each other to maintain the correct balance. Try to relax into the stretch – there should be no tension anywhere else in the body. You can bring your hands to rest on the abdomen so that the shoulder blades may widen and the elbows release.

2 Work up to spending five minutes there. Slowly bring your thighs together and give your inner thighs a good rub!

3 Should you wish to increase the stretch, you can place leg weights on your inner thighs.

4 Make sure that your pelvis stays in neutral.

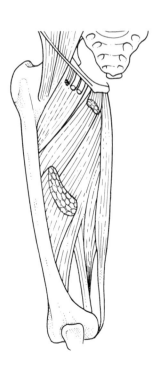

The muscles of the inner thigh – the adductors

EXERCISE 35

Standing Quadriceps Stretch (all levels)

Aim

To stretch the front of the thighs (quadriceps, see illustration on page 116).

Please take advice if you have a knee injury.

Equipment

A scarf (optional, see Watchpoints below).

Starting Position

▷ Stand alongside the wall placing your left hand on the wall for support and remembering all the directions for Standing correctly (page 93).

Action

1 Breathe in to prepare and lengthen up through the spine.
2 Breathe out, zip up and hollow, and bend the right knee so that you may clasp your ankle with your right hand. As you do so, check that you have not

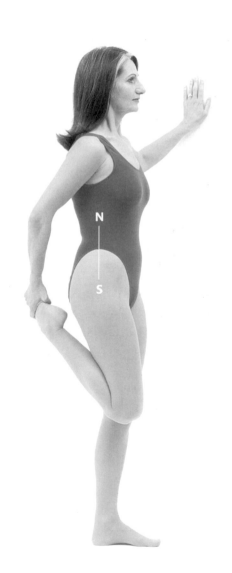

Full position

arched or bowed your back – it must stay neutral. Imagine that there is a small weight attached to your tailbone helping to keep the length at the base of the spine.

3 Gently pull the knee towards your buttock, keeping the knee still and in line with your other leg. Do not take it too far back. Keep lengthening from the top of your head to your tailbone.

4 Hold the stretch while breathing normally for thirty seconds.

5 Repeat twice on each leg.

Watchpoints

▷ If you know that you are not flexible or you have a knee problem, use a long scarf to help. Place it over the front of your foot, hold it with the right hand and gently bring your foot towards your bottom.

▷ The most common mistake made with this exercise is to allow the pelvis to shift as the leg bends back. Keep the tailbone lengthening downwards towards the floor and maintain the natural curve of the spine.

Like so many people, my work entails remaining seated for long periods, without the opportunity even to walk around the 'office'. This frequently leads to muscular aches and pains, and an associated loss of suppleness. Pilates enables me to exercise virtually anywhere, at any time – even in my seat. When I get to my hotel, the full range of Pilates exercises are easily completed in the privacy of my own room, in a relaxing environment and without any special equipment.

I recommend Body Control Pilates to all my colleagues and to anyone else who wants to maximize their body's 'potential'.

Sean Volrath, Boeing 747 *Classic* Pilot

Barre Exercises (all levels)

Aim

To strengthen the leg muscles, especially the quadriceps and, in particular, the vastus medialis. To learn correct alignment of the legs. To achieve pelvic stability.

These traditional barre exercises are a great workout for the legs and are proof that you do not need expensive or elaborate equipment to achieve results.

Alignment is everything for this exercise. By bending the knee correctly over the foot and keeping

Starting position

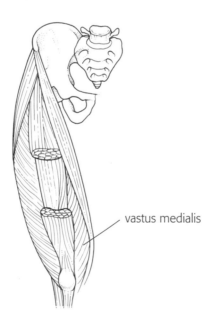

vastus medialis

The quadriceps at the front of your thigh

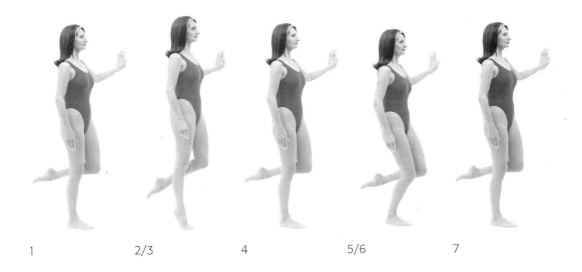

| 1 | 2/3 | 4 | 5/6 | 7 |

it directly over the second toe, you are working the thigh muscles as nature intended. Deviate just a little and you have the potential for an imbalance which, if it became habitual, could lead to knee problems.

The group of muscles known collectively as the quadriceps are, as one would expect from the name, made up of four muscles. If one of these four becomes dominant, the delicate balance is upset and the knee joint is compromised. The muscle most likely to weaken is vastus medialis, the main stabilizer of the knee joint. It has its own blood supply and begins to waste after just twenty-four hours of bed rest!

You must also pay close attention to your pelvis in this exercise. It must stay level as you bend the knee, as this keeps its stability. Allow it to dip, and it's gone – the Preparatory Exercise we have given you will help you achieve this. Do not proceed to the main exercise until you have mastered keeping the pelvis level.

Starting Position and Preparatory Exercise

▷ Stand side on to the wall, remembering to lengthen up through the spine, but don't hold on to the wall just yet.

▷ Zipping and hollowing, bend the leg closest to the wall, so that the knee faces straight forward and the foot is resting just beside the other knee. As you do so make sure that your pelvis stays level and doesn't dip or twist or tilt (see above).

▷ Now you may hold on to the wall for support.

Action

1 Breathe in and lengthen up through the spine.

2 Breathe out, zipping up and hollowing, and rise up on to your toes.

The knee bends directly over the second toe

3 Breathe in.

4 Breathe out, zipping up and hollowing, and slowly bring your heel back down on to the floor. Think of the heel lengthening away from the top of your head. It is as if your head stays up there at the higher level!

5 Now breathe in wide and full.

6 Breathe out, still zipped and hollowed, and bend your knee, bringing the kneecap **directly over the centre of your foot**. As you do so, do not sink into your hips but keep lengthening up and **keep your pelvis level.**

7 Breathe in and straighten the leg.

8 Repeat five times on each leg, turning

Watchpoints

▷ Make sure that your knee goes directly over the centre of the foot.

▷ Do not allow your foot or ankle to roll inwards as you bend the knee.

▷ Do not bend the knee until your heel is fully lowered.

▷ Make sure your pelvis stays level.

Strong centre – long waist

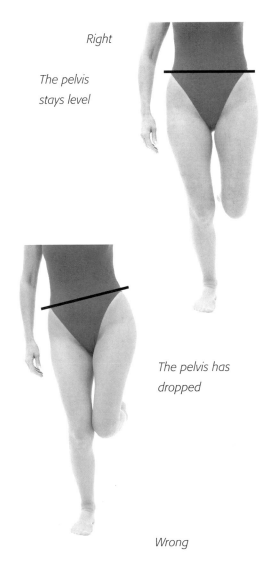

Right

The pelvis stays level

The pelvis has dropped

Wrong

around so that your bent knee is next to the wall. Do not allow your bottom to stick out. Think of the weight on your tailbone.

The Flexible Spine

Pilates has changed my life. I've gone from needing weekly visits to the osteopath, to having complete confidence in my own body. Before Pilates classes with Lynne, I was afraid to do even the most gentle of daily tasks in case I put my back out. Now my whole posture has changed, I am stronger, leaner and fitter than I've ever been. I feel and look great. And I haven't seen the osteopath for months.

Shelley Sishton (Marketing Consultant)

If your spine is inflexibly stiff at thirty, you are old. If it is completely flexible at sixty, you are young.

Joseph Pilates

When rising from the floor or lowering yourself to the floor, always do so with a 'rolling' or 'unrolling' motion exactly in the imitation of a wheel, equipped with imaginary 'vertebra' rolling forward or backward. Vertebra by vertebra try to 'roll' or 'unroll'.

Joseph Pilates

Take a moment to consider just what your spine does for you each and every day.

Among other things:

▷ It allows for movement – forwards, backwards and sideways.
▷ It protects the spinal cord.
▷ It supports the head.
▷ It acts like a ship's mast, providing rigidity to maintain upright posture.
▷ The discs between the vertebrae act as shock absorbers.

▷ The red bone marrow within it forms blood cells.

Yet we hardly give it a thought. Many factors contribute to the ill health of our spine. One of the main problems is that localized areas of the spine can become locked, the most common being the mid-thoracic (between your shoulder blades) and the lumbar spine (low back).

In a healthy back all the different segments of the spine work together to create the desired move-ment, each vertebra contributing to that movement – a little like a bicycle chain. When one level is

The Cervical Spine: the most mobile of all the spinal areas permitting all movements.

The Thoracic Spine: this is the least mobile of all the spinal areas due to the attachment of the ribs. There is little ability to bend forward or backward, but if you wish to twist or rotate, most of the action will take place here, especially in the section just above the hollow of your back.

The Lumbar Spine: here, rotation is very limited, but forward and backward bending (flexion and extension) occur mainly from this area.

Sacrum

The movement potential of your spine will depend on your posture.

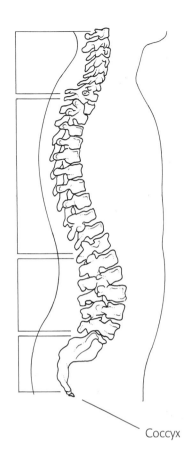

Coccyx

locked, the 'chain' is upset. What often happens then is that the levels above and below the locked area become over-flexible to compensate for the area that will not move – you can be hypo-mobile (not enough movement) in one area and hyper-mobile (too much movement) above, and/or below. This puts enormous strain on the back.

One of the main goals of Pilates is to stabilize the spine, engaging tranversus abdominis and multifidus. Once stable, the inflexible areas can become more mobile and the over-mobile areas more stable. When this happens the spine can move again, 'like a wheel', vertebra by vertebra as it is stabilized at an intervertebral level. The first step is always to stabilize and zip up and hollow.

Many Pilates exercises work toward this goal. Exercises such as Spine Curls (page 44) and Roll Downs (page 152) encourage this segmental control. We have also chosen exercises to make the spine more flexible.

Spine Curls with Marching Feet (intermediate level)

Aim

To use the spine like a wheel to achieve segmental control. To learn pelvic stability, combining this with 'functional' movement. To work the deep stabilizers and tone the buttocks. To improve co-ordination and foot control.

This is a wonderful example of how you can progress with Pilates. The exercise requires you to draw on skills already learnt in other exercises in order to perform a complex movement sequence.

It's a good idea to practise Spine Curls with or without squeezing the pillow first to prepare the spine.

Equipment

A firm flat pillow (optional).

Action 1

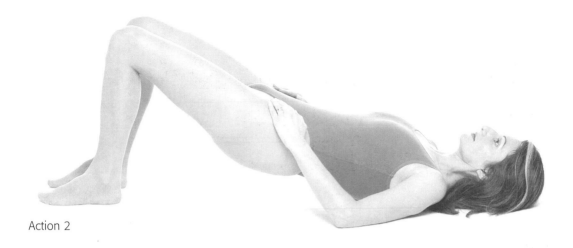

Action 2

Starting Position

▷ Lie on your back with your feet flat on
the floor, in parallel and hip-width
apart, about 30 centimetres from your
buttocks. Use a firm flat pillow under
your head if necessary.

▷ Have your arms by your sides but
place the hands on your pelvis. The
elbows stay on the floor.

Action

1   Breathe in wide and full to prepare.

2   Breathe out, zip up and hollow, and
wheel the spine off the floor, bone by
bone. If possible curl up to your
shoulder blade area, but not higher.

3   Breathing normally now and
continuing to zip up and hollow,
engage your buttocks and lift the toes
of one foot off the floor so that you

Action 3

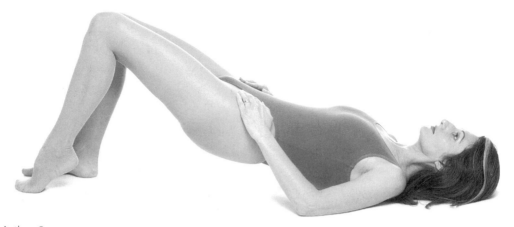

Action 6

come on to your heels. Place them back down and repeat with the other foot. The pelvis stays still.

4   Repeat five times with each foot, keeping the pelvis where it is and totally still, square and stable!

5   When you have finished, breathe out, zip up and hollow, and slowly lower, bone by bone.

6   You are now going to repeat the same thing, but this time lifting alternate

heels off the floor. Once again, do not allow the pelvis to sink back down or move. Your hands can help you to stabilize.

7   When you have mastered this, you can really show off by lifting opposite heels and toes, keeping the pelvis up there and stable.

8   At the end of the series of movements, move on to the Hip Flexer Stretch over.

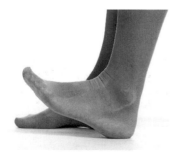

Full Action. 3 Toe lifted

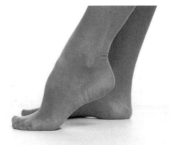

6 Heel lifted

7 Opposite toe and heel lifted

Watchpoints

▷ You must not arch the back. Keep in your mind the image of a whippet who has just been scolded and has his tail (your tailbone) curled between his legs!

▷ Keep your neck long and soft.

▷ Don't forget to zip up and hollow throughout.

▷ Always lower the spine, bone by bone, lengthening it away.

The Hip Flexer Stretch

To finish

A nice way to finish this exercise is with a Hip Flexer Stretch.

Action

1 Breathe in wide and full.

2 Breathe out, zip and hollow and fold one knee onto your chest. Take hold of it with both hands, holding it underneath the thigh if you have a knee injury.

3 Breathe in.

4 Breathe out, zip and hollow and slide the other leg along the floor. Stay neutral.

Take 5 breaths in this position – shoulders down into your back, elbows open, neck released. Repeat on the other side.

Hip Flexer Stretch

Spine Stretch (intermediate level)

Aim

To·gently stretch the spine and the inner thighs (adductors). To focus on lateral lower ribcage breathing. To stabilize the trunk.

This exercise is really a follow-on from the static stretches at the beginning of the book in the Warming Up chapter but it offers more of a stretch and, therefore, is not appropriate at the start of a session. It is very important to have stability before you try to stretch.

The wider you place your legs the greater the stretch, but this depends on the flexibility of your hips. Please do not overstretch.

Starting Position

▷ Sit on your sitting bones with your legs in front of you. If you like you may sit on a rolled-up towel – it will help you to keep your pelvis at the right angle. You could also try sitting with your buttocks up against the wall.

Starting position

▷ Take your legs a comfortable distance apart. Do not force the knees down into the floor, they may remain a little bent if necessary. Have your toes softly pointed until you are very flexible, at which point you can have your feet flexed.

Action

1 Breathe in to prepare and lift up out of the hips and lengthen up through the spine. Imagine that there is a pole behind you along your spine. Lengthen up along that pole.

2 Breathe out, zip up and hollow, and drop your chin forward, gently tucking it in. Then, like a roller blind, curl downwards, aiming the top of your head towards the centre of your stomach. Reach forward with your hands.

3 Continue to breathe normally and, maintaining the zip and hollow, inch forward reaching through the fingers. If you are flexible enough, try to press your knees into the floor, lengthening through the heels.

4 After eight breaths, zipped and hollowed still, slowly start to unfurl, restacking the vertebrae one on top of the other until the spinal column is rebuilt along the length of the imaginary pole. Bring your head up last of all.

5 Repeat three times.

Watchpoints

▷ Keep your shoulders down into your back and your neck long and released.

▷ Keep breathing into the back of your ribcage.

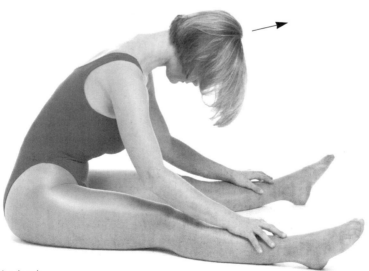

Breathing into the back

EXERCISE 39

The Saw (advanced level)

Aim

This exercise works on many levels, but its main aims are to stretch your spine, sides, inner thighs and hamstrings, while stabilizing.

All the previous exercises will have prepared your body for this lovely classic Pilates exercise, so that you may perform it with grace and ease! You will notice that there are some fairly complicated instructions in the Action section below. It would be wise to read them through first a couple of times and study the photos before you begin.

Note: As this exercise involves bending forward and rotating the spine, anyone with back problems should consult their specialist before attempting it.

Starting Position

▷ Sit on your sitting bones with your legs in front of you. If you like, you may sit on a rolled-up towel as it will help you to keep your pelvis at the right angle.

▷ Take your legs a comfortable distance

apart, do not force the knees down into the floor, they may remain a little bent, if necessary. Have your toes softly pointed until you are very flexible, at which point you can have your feet flexed.

Action

1 Breathe in to prepare and lengthen the spine up the imaginary pole.
2 Bring your arms up to your sides, parallel to the floor like aeroplane wings, with the palms down. You are reaching through the fingertips. Your shoulder blades stay down into your back.
3 Breathe out, zip up and hollow, and rotate your body to the right so that you are facing your right leg.

Action 2

4 Breathe in and lengthen up again.

Action 3

5

Breathe out, still zipped and hollowed, and rotate to the right some more, at the same time reaching forward and down so that the edge of your left hand slides down to the outside of the little toe of your right foot. It is as if you are going to saw the toe off! As your left arm reaches forward, stretch your right arm out behind you, raising it as high as possible like a wing, the palm facing backwards. The shoulder blade stays down. You will be looking over your shoulder. The back of your neck stays long. Your buttocks are glued to the floor!

6 Take two breaths in this position, then return on the out-breath by reversing the instructions. Remember to lengthen and pause before you return to centre.

7 Repeat five times to each side.

Watchpoints

▷ Remember to keep hollowing navel to spine throughout.

▷ Both buttocks stay on the floor.

▷ Your neck stays long and released and your shoulder blades stay down into your back.

Action 5

Rolling like a Ball (intermediate level)

Aim

To massage the spine, making it both flexible and strong. To strengthen the deep abdominals. To control your body and have fun!

You must be on a thick mat or a thick blanket for this one, especially if you have a bony spine. At first you will probably go 'ker-clunk' rather than rolling like a ball but as your spine becomes more flexible, you should be able to feel the wheeling effect. The secret is to use your deep abdominals, rather than mere momentum, to roll.

Please do not get carried away and do a backward somersault! You shouldn't come on to the neck or the head. It's a good idea to move any antiques, small children or animals out of the way though, just in case!

Please take advice if you have disc or spinal problems. Avoid if you have osteoporosis.

Action 1

Starting Position

▷ Sit on the mat and bring your knees in close to you.

▷ Hold your legs just under the knees on the back of your thighs.

▷ Tuck in your chin.

Action 3

Action

1 Breathe in to prepare.
2 Breathe out, zip up and hollow.
3 Breathe in and roll backwards on to your shoulders, not your neck.
4 Keep hold of your legs and keep your chin tucked in.
5 Breathe out, still zipped and hollowed, and roll back up again.
6 Repeat eight times.

Variation One

▷ When you are more in control, try not putting your feet back on the floor when you return to upright. You'll need to work your abdominals harder to achieve that.

Variation Two

▷ Hug your knees to you and hold your ankles. Your heels should stay close to your buttocks.

Watchpoints

▷ Do not come too far back or you may hurt your neck.

▷ Keep using those abdominals.

▷ Keep your chin tucked in.

Action 3 continued

The Seal (intermediate)

Aim

To learn co-ordination and control. To work the abdominals. To massage the spine. To entertain onlookers!

If you thought that the last exercise was fun, then you'll love this one. It is best done in a darkened room with the curtains pulled!

Please take advice if you have a spinal or disc-related problem. Avoid if you have osteoporosis.

Starting Position

▷ Sit with your feet on your mat. Have your heels together, toes apart.

▷ Take your arms in front of you and down through the inside of your legs and around the back of your ankles to hold the ankles in the front. See the photo!

▷ Gently tuck in your chin.

Action 2

Flap your feet like flippers

Action 2 continued

Action

1 Breathe in to prepare.
2 Breathe out, zip up and hollow, and roll backwards as for the previous exercise. When back, flap your feet together twice like flippers. The heels stay together.
3 Breathe in, still zipped and hollowed and, as you roll back upright again, don't put your feet on the floor but flap them again like flippers.
4 Repeat five times.

Now you know why it's called The Seal!!!

Watchpoints

▷ Use your abdominals throughout.
▷ Do not roll too far back.
▷ Keep your chin tucked in.

Action 3

Increasing the Load

Two years ago before starting Pilates with Lynne, I frequently spent two days out of seven lying flat on my back. I tried physiotherapy, rest, sclerosant injections and a back corset, but nothing seemed to remedy the problem. Pilates taught me to stabilize so that I had my own 'natural back support'. Now I'm back riding, cycling and I even went skiing this year with no ill effects. Now, if I feel a twinge, I know that wherever I am, I can do half an hour of Pilates exercises and immediately feel the benefits.

Lucy Wigley (Nursery Carer and keen horsewoman)

In everyday life we are constantly lifting heavy loads, therefore we need to learn how to do this safely using the right muscles and, of course, stabilizing.

There is an additional reason why we should work out using weights. From about our mid thirties on, our bones begin to lose calcium and become thinner, which leaves us, both men and women, prone to osteoporosis (thinning of the bones). Although it looks very solid, bone is, in fact, full of holes rather like coral. Bone health is determined by nutrition, mineral and vitamin content and, also, by the amount of stress it is put under. This is one type of stress that is good for us! Bones become thicker and stronger when they are stressed, as stresses produce electrical effects which in turn encourages growth. If there is no stress, then the bone will be less dense and weaker.

Menopausal women in particular have an accelerated bone loss, which comes with the decline in the ovarian hormone, oestrogen. Fractures caused by osteoporosis are a major risk for the elderly. One in three women over 50 in Britain will fracture their wrist, hip or spine, and one in five of these will die within a year of the accident.

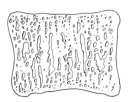

Healthy bone

Brittle bone

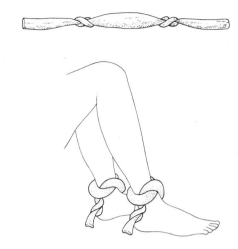

Making the weights

Fortunately, bone density responds very well to weight-bearing exercise. Recent research has shown that regular exercise, weight-training and a calcium-rich diet can not only help to prevent brittle bones, but can also help to reverse the damage. We shouldn't wait until we are older to work on our bones, and even teenagers should consider adding light weights to their exercise programme.

If you are concerned that you may end up looking like Arnold Schwarzenegger, fear not, for in Pilates we use only light weights up to 2 to 2.5 kilograms. They help to tone the muscles and build bone density but will not 'bulk' the muscles – remember our goal is strength and flexibility. If you do want to look like Arnold Schwarzenegger, you can, if you wish, use heavier weights as long as you apply the Eight Principles. You will also need to watch your muscle balance, paying particular attention to your suppleness or you may become muscle-bound.

All of the following exercises can be done without any weights at all. In fact, we even recommend that you first attempt them without weights to perfect your technique and slowly build your muscle strength. When you are confident, then you can start to use home-made weights, such as a small can of beans or a bag of rice and then work up to larger tin or pack sizes. We believe that you should only invest in buying weights when you are comfortable with the exercises.

If you don't have a set of leg weights, take an old, clean pair of thick tights and cut the legs off. About 15 centimetres from the toes, tie a knot. Weigh out between 0.5 to 1 kilogram of rice (uncooked!) and pour it into the tights. Tie another knot about 20 centimetres away from the first knot. Now you have a set of weights which you can tie on to your ankles. A word of caution. Make sure that you pick a pair of tights with no holes or all the rice trickles through!

As you become more comfortable with using weights you can increase the weight. Up to 2.5 kilogram for each arm weight is suitable and up to 1 kilogram for each leg weight.

The Wrist Worker (all levels)

Aim

To strengthen the hands, wrists, forearms and upper arms, maintaining good posture.

This one looks easy, but it's deceptive as you really do work the whole arm.

Steps to make the wrist-worker

You will need to make a wrist-worker. It's very simple. Take approximately a 45 centimetre length of dowel (wooden pole) which is about 2.5 centimetres in diameter. Drill a hole through the centre and thread through a piece of rope which is about 1.5 metres long, tying a knot so that it is firmly secured. To the other end of the rope, you can attach a weight. You could use an old pair of tights or socks (clean) or a bag filled with beans (dried, not baked) or rice, or you could buy a beanbag. The weight should be between 0.5 to 1.5 kilograms.

The idea is that you start with the rope fully wound around the stick, then slowly unwind it before winding it up again.

Please take advice if you are prone to tennis or golfer's elbow.

Starting Position

▷ Stand correctly, remembering all the directions given on page 93.
▷ Hold the wrist-worker out in front of you at shoulder height, with your arms straight but not locked and parallel to the floor. Hold the dowel from underneath with the palms facing upwards, hands on either side of the rope.
▷ Breathe normally throughout.

Rolling down

Rolling up

Action

1 Before you begin, lengthen up through the spine and zip up and hollow.

2 As you unravel the rope make the wrists work alternately. Rotate the stick towards you as though you were wringing it out. The stick will rotate in the palm of the other hand. Make sure that your shoulder blades stay down into your back and your neck and upper shoulders stay soft and relaxed.

3 When fully unravelled, change the hand position so that you are holding the dowel from above, with the palms facing down, as you roll the rope back up again. This time the stick rotates away from you.

4 Once is enough for this exercise. When it becomes easier you may place a heavier weight in the bag.

So, to recap:

5 Palms facing up as the rope unwinds down.

6 Palms facing down as the rope winds back up.

Watchpoints

▷ Don't let your shoulders creep up around your ears. Keep them soft and down.

▷ Keep your arms straight out in front of you. Don't let them drop.

▷ Don't skimp on the wrist movement. Make a full turn.

Working the Triceps (all levels)

Aim

To strengthen the triceps without compromising the neck. If using a cushion, to strengthen the inner thighs.

There are lots of ways to work the triceps. This one is great because there is no risk of overusing your neck muscles. You will need to take a firm grip on the weight, unless you are after the broken-nose look (very popular with some Pilates teachers!!!).

Equipment

A weight of between 1 and 3 kilograms. You can either buy a long hand-held weight or use a tall can or a heavy rolling pin. Obviously start with the lightest weight and work up. You may also need a cushion or tennis ball.

Starting Position

▷ Lie with your knees bent, the pelvis in neutral. If you wish, you may place a small cushion or tennis ball between your knees and throughout the exercise you can squeeze the cushion to work the inner thighs.

▷ Hold the weight at each end, with your palms facing upwards. Your elbows are bent directly over your shoulders. Your upper arms are vertical to you.

Action

1 Breathe in to prepare.
2 Breathe out, zip up and hollow, and slowly bend the arms lowering the

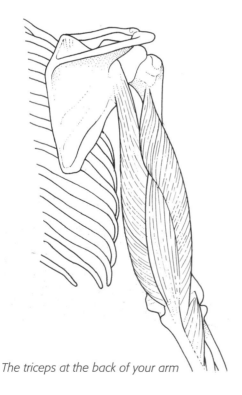

The triceps at the back of your arm

weight down just above your head.
Keeping the elbow quite still.

3 Breathe in as you slowly straighten
the arms – do not lock the elbows.

4 Repeat up to twenty times.

Watchpoints

▷ Keep that firm grip on the weight.
▷ Keep your neck released and your
shoulder blades down into your back.
▷ If you are squeezing the cushion
between your knees, be sure that you
do not tilt the pelvis or grip around
the hips (see the Pillow Squeeze,
page 42).

Starting position

Full position – the elbows stay still

EXERCISE 44

The Albatross
(intermediate level)

Starting position

Aim

To strengthen the upper back muscles, stabilize the shoulder blades and strengthen the muscles of the arms.

This is an exercise commonly seen in gyms throughout the country. The key to doing it correctly lies in the awareness of the spine lengthening and the stabilizing muscles working. You must also concentrate on the muscles between the shoulder blades and on working the deep neck flexors.

Please take advice if you have back problems.

Equipment

You will need a pair of hand-held weights or, otherwise, use two tins. You should start with a 0.5 kilogram weight and work up to 2.5 kilograms per weight.

Starting Position

▷   Holding your weights, stand with your feet just wider than hip-width apart. Bend your knees and, zipped up and

Full position

Action

1 Breathe in to prepare and lengthen through the spine.

2 Breathe out, zip up and hollow, and bring your arms to a level with your shoulders. The elbows remain softly bent so that the arms maintain their natural curve. Think of bringing your shoulder blades together. They, of course, remain down into your back.

3 Breathe in and return the arms to the Starting Position.

4 Repeat up to ten times.

Watchpoints

▷ Keep the neck lengthening, do not tip your head back.

▷ Keep the curve in your arms.

▷ Be aware of the movement of your shoulder blades back and together but staying down in your back.

hollowed, bend your body forward from your hips.

▷ Throughout the exercise keep lengthening from the top of your head to your tailbone, and keep zipping up and hollowing. Choose a spot on the floor to focus on so that the back of your neck remains long.

▷ Your arms are held in front of you as if you are hugging the trunk of a tree.

Advanced Version

▷ To work that little bit harder, take an extra breath.

▷ Breathe in and lengthen through the spine.

▷ Breathe out, zip up and hollow, and bring the arms back.

▷ Breathe in and hold.

▷ Breathe out and lower.

The Hinge (all levels)

Aim

To work the triceps and the wrist. Take advice if you have a back problem.

Equipment

One hand-held weight or a tin from the store cupboard up to 0.5 to 1.5 kilograms.

Starting position

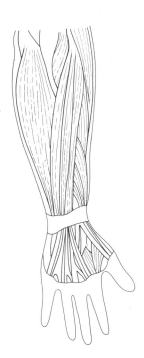

Wrist flexors and extensors

Starting Position

▷ Stand facing a table or a wall with one hand on the table to steady you. Your feet hip-width apart, your knees bent and your body pivoted forward from the hips. Remember to stay zipped up and hollowed.

▷ Your back is lengthening from the top of your head to your tailbone. The back of your neck is long.

▷ Hold the weight in one hand and your elbow bent close in to you.

Action 2

Watchpoints

▷ Keep lengthening through the spine and zipping up and hollowing.

▷ Be careful not to twist in the wrist in and out away from the mid-line, the weight goes straight back.

Action 5. Adding the wrist action

Action

1 Breathe in to prepare and lengthen through the spine.

2 Breathe out, zip up and hollow, and straighten your arm, hinging from the elbow. The elbow itself remains quite still.

3 Breathe in as you return the arm.

4 Repeat ten times.

Adding the Wrist

▷ Follow the first two action points above.

5 Breathe in and lengthen the wrist as in the third position above.

6 Breathe out as you bend the arm again.

7 Repeat five times with each wrist.

The Feet and Hands

The Feet

Aim

To work the arches of the feet and the deep stabilising muscles such as the lumbricales and interossei.

Action

Sit or stand, your feet flat on the floor.

▷ Draw the base of your toes back towards your heels, keeping the toes long and the base of the toes down on the floor. Release. It might give you cramp; if it does, just rest a minute before continuing.

▷ Repeat ten times.

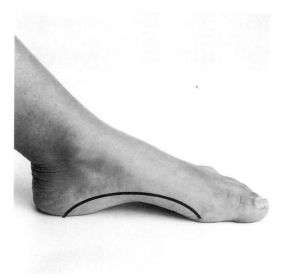
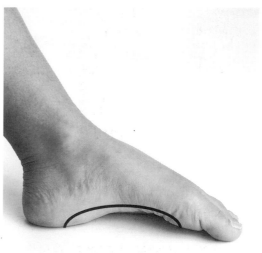

Hands

You can do this exercise for the hands as well.

To keep your hands supple and strong, invest in some children's playdough and some Chinese balls!

Squeezing the dough while watching TV or reading is very therapeutic and strengthens the hands and grip.

The Chinese balls are rotated in the hands which improves your dexterity and keeps your fingers mobile!

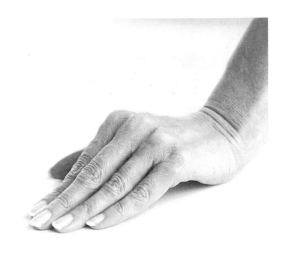

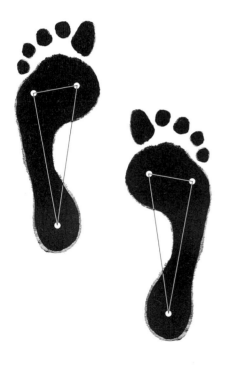

True flexibility can be acheived only when all the muscles are uniformly developed.

Joseph Pilates

Always stand with the weight evenly balanced on your feet – imagine a triangle – base of the big toe, base of the small toe and the centre of the heel – keep your weight centred on the triangles.

EXERCISE 47

Passé Développés (intermediate)

Aim

To achieve the correct balance in the leg, hip and buttock muscles. To learn stability of the pelvis. To work the muscles which turn the leg out from the hip (lateral rotators). To achieve control of the muscles around the hip joint. In order to straighten the leg, your hamstrings must be the correct length which is why this exercise is at an intermediate level.

For this exercise we would normally use a triangular cushion made from foam which offers just the right amount of support for the spine. If you cannot get hold of one, use a couple of pillows.

Remember the exercise on Stabilizing the Pelvis (page 50). You are going to do the same action now, turning out the leg from the hip without losing the stability of the pelvis.

Practise the exercises without weights to begin with – then, when you are ready, attach the weights to your ankles.

Please take advice if you suffer from sciatica.

Equipment

A triangular cushion or large pillow.
Leg weights, each 0.5 to 1.5 kilograms maximum in weight.

Action 1

Starting Position

▷ Lie on the cushion or pillow. The idea is that your upper back is supported, but your lower ribcage, waist and pelvis are on the mat. Above all, you should feel comfortable and not scrunched up.

▷ Your knees are bent hip-width apart and in parallel.

Action

1 Breathe in to prepare.
2 Breathe out, zip up and hollow, and fold your knee up, then turn it out from the hip, without moving the pelvis.
3 Breathe in, still zipped and hollowed, and slowly straighten the leg, keeping it turned out from the hip but in a line with your hip. Keep your tailbone on the floor.

Action 2

4 Breathe out and, when the leg is straight, flex the foot.

5 Then, zipped and hollowed, lower the leg, which should still be turned out, and flex the foot down almost to touch the floor. As you lower, keep lengthening down the inside of the leg through the heel but keep the top of the thigh bone anchored into the hip socket. Do not allow the back to arch.

Action 2 continued

Action 3/4

6 Breathe in and turn the leg into parallel from the hip, so that the kneecap faces up. Softly point the foot.

7 Breathe out, still zipped and hollowed, and bend the knee in again. Turn it out from the hip and repeat the last three movements.

8 Repeat ten times with each leg.

Action 5

Watchpoints

▷ The most important aspect of this exercise is to keep the pelvis stable. Do not allow it to move from its neutral position. It should not tilt at all either to the north, south, east or west!

▷ Think of keeping the length and width in the front of your pelvis to stop you from scrunching up.

▷ Do not flex the foot until the leg is fully straightened.

▷ Keep the leg in line with the hip. Do not allow it to go outside your body width.

▷ Keep the other foot flat on the floor.

▷ Keep lengthening through the heel of the foot as you lower the leg.

Battement (intermediate)

Aim

To teach stability in the pelvis while moving the legs. To strengthen the muscles which turn the leg out from the hip (lateral rotators).

You need to be able to straighten your leg comfortably into the air for this exercise. If this is difficult for you, please continue with the other exercises, especially the Studio Stretches on page 34 until you are ready. Remember that the whole leg must be turned out from the hip joint itself.

Please take advice if you suffer from sciatica.

Equipment

As for Passé Développés

Starting Position

▷ Lie on your cushion or pillow as for the previous exercise.

▷ Straighten one leg out in front of you, turned out from the hip with the foot softly pointed at a 45° angle. The other leg remains bent, with the foot planted on the floor.

Action 3. Raise the leg, toe pointed, leg turned out

Action

1 Breathe in to prepare.
2 Breathe out, zip up and hollow.
3 Breathe in and raise the leg into the air, keeping it turned out and straight. Keep your pelvis stable, your tailbone down.
4 Breathe out, zipping and hollowing, and flex the foot. Slowly lower the leg almost to the floor. Lengthen down the inside of the leg through the heel.
5 Breathe in, softly point the foot and raise the leg again.
6 Repeat ten times with each leg.
7 When you are confident with the movements, aim to raise the leg to a count of two and lower it to a count of four.

Action 4. Flex the foot

Watchpoints

▷ Keep the pelvis steady and square.
▷ Don't let the stomach muscles bulge.
▷ The tailbone stays down!
▷ The head of the thigh bone stays anchored into the hip socket.

Action 4. Lower the leg

Small Circles (intermediate)

Aim

To strengthen the muscles around the hip. To learn fine control of the muscles around the hip. To stabilize the pelvis.

Please remember that we are looking for circles, not stars or squares or pentagons. Circles!

Please take advice before starting if you suffer from sciatica.

Draw tiny circles, lengthening through the heel

Equipment

As for Passé Développés.

Starting Position

▷ Lie on your pillow or cushion, as for the previous two exercises.

Action

1 Breathe in to prepare.
2 Breathe out, zipping up and hollowing, and bend and straighten one leg into the air above your hip. Hold the leg at an angle (see photo).
3 Breathing normally now, turn the leg out from your hip, keeping the pelvis stable. Flex the foot and slowly draw small circles in the air with the whole leg – imagine you are drawing the circle with your heel.
4 Draw ten circles in each direction with each leg.

Watchpoints

▷ Keep lengthening through the heel and the inside of the leg.
▷ Keep the leg anchored into the hip socket.
▷ Keep breathing.
▷ Keep hollowing to stabilize the pelvis.
▷ Keep the leg anchored into the hip joint – it should feel heavy.
▷ Keep the circles very small and very circular!
▷ Don't let the leg drop away from you.

As an architect, writer and traveller my attachment to Pilates is one based on the sanity and balance it provides to the madness, deadline and stress about us. The concentration and quiet the exercises demand becomes a ritual both the body and the mind thrive on, to contain and sustain the inner being . . . . Pilates for the past ten years has been an essential and precious part of my life, a rewarding contribution resulting in the line and flexibility I have developed and maintain. At forty something, an invaluable source of pride.

Salma Samar Damlutji, AA Dipl. PhD (RCA)

Winding Down

For the last ten years I have suffered from severe back pain following an injury on duty as a police officer. This problem has impacted upon my career and quality of life as I have struggled to overcome the condition. On the advice of my doctor and osteopath I took up a weekly class of Pilates exercises with Lynne. The impact on my pain and resulting poor posture was immediate, and there has been steady improvement since. Pilates for me has meant less time off work, an ability to reduce back pain and given me a more active and happier life.

Marshall Kent (Police Officer working in an inner city)

It is always a good idea to warm down gently after a session, although in truth, it is very rare to feel stiff or uncomfortable the day after a Pilates session because you have been working slowly with such careful control.

Most people find this section the best bit of the workout, as you can really relax knowing that your body is balanced and centred. Use the following exercises on their own for relaxation if you are feeling particularly stressed.

EXERCISE 50

Roll Downs (all levels)

Aim

To release tension in the spine, the shoulders and the upper body. To mobilize the spine, creating flexibility and strength and achieving segmental control.

To teach the correct use of stabilizing abdominals when bending.

A core exercise in any Pilates programme, this can be used as a warm-up or a wind down. It combines stabilizing work with the wonderful

Start to roll down –
remember you zip and hollow

wheeling motion of the spine. As you roll back up, think of rebuilding the spinal column, stacking each vertebra one on top of the other to lengthen out the spine.

Please take advice if you have a back problem, especially if this is disc-related. Avoid this exercise if you have osteoporosis.

The exercise can be done freestanding or leaning into a wall – we've shown you both versions.

Starting Position

▷ Stand with your feet hip-width apart and in parallel with your weight evenly balanced on both feet. Check that you are not rolling your feet in or out. Soften your knees.

▷ Find your neutral pelvis position, but keep the tailbone lengthening down.

Action

1 Breathe in to prepare and lengthen up through the spine, release the head and neck.

2 Breathe out, zip up and hollow, and drop your chin on to your chest and allow the weight of your head to make you slowly roll forward, head released, arms hanging, centre strong, knees soft.

3 Breathe in as you hang, really letting your head and arms hang.

4 Breathe out, firmly zipped up and hollowed, as you drop your tailbone down, directing your pubic bone forward. Rotate your pelvis backwards as you slowly come up, rolling through the spine bone by bone, to stand tall.

5 Repeat six times.

Watchpoints

▷ You may like to take an extra breath during the exercise. This is fine, but please try to breathe out as you move the spine.

▷ Make sure that you go down centrally and that you do not sway over to one side. When you are down, check where your hands are in relation to your feet.

▷ Do not roll the feet in or out. Keep the weight evenly balanced and try not to lean forward on to the front of your feet or back on to the heels.

Drop your tailbone down, direct your pubic bone forward and rotate the pelvis, unfurling the spine bone by bone

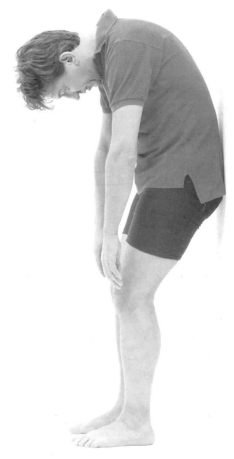

Rolling Down the Wall

Rolling Down the Wall (all levels)

If you have a back problem, you may feel more secure rolling down the wall.

▷ To use the wall, stand about eighteen inches from it and lean back into it, with knees bent. You should look like you are sitting on a bar stool! Feet in parallel please.

▷ Follow the instructions as above, but start by sliding your hands down your thighs.

▷ Try to place your spine back on to the wall bone by bone.

Arm Openings (all levels)

Aim

To wind down the body by relaxing the upper body while opening the chest. To achieve a sense of openness while stabilizing and centring. To gently rotate the spine.

This has to be the most relaxing, feel-good exercise in the Pilates programme. It is perfect to do at the end of the day, especially if you have been sitting at a desk. The great thing is that you are also working hard.

Be completely aware of your arm and hand as it displaces the air moving through space.

As this exercise involves rotation of the spine, please take advice if you have a disc-related injury.

Equipment

A pillow – a bed pillow is perfect.

Starting Position

▷ Lie on your side with your head on a pillow and knees curled up at a right angle to your body. Your back should be in a straight line, but with its natural curve, of course.

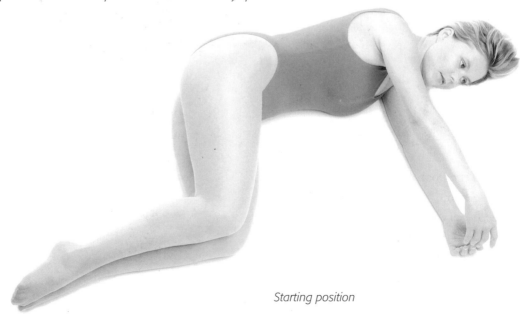

Starting position

▷ Line all your bones up. Both feet and ankle bones, both knee and hip bones, and both shoulders should be on top of each other.

▷ Your arms are extended in front of you with palms together at shoulder height.

Action

1 Breathe in to prepare and lengthen through the spine.

2 Breathe out and zip up and hollow.

3 Breathe in as you slowly extend and lift the upper arm, keeping the elbow soft, opening out like a door. Keep your eyes on your hand so that the head follows the arm movement. You are aiming to

touch the floor behind you, but do not force it. Try to keep your knees together, your pelvis still. Stay zipped and hollowed.

4 Breathe out as you bring the arm back in an arc to rest on the other hand again.

5 Repeat five times, then curl up on the other side and start again.

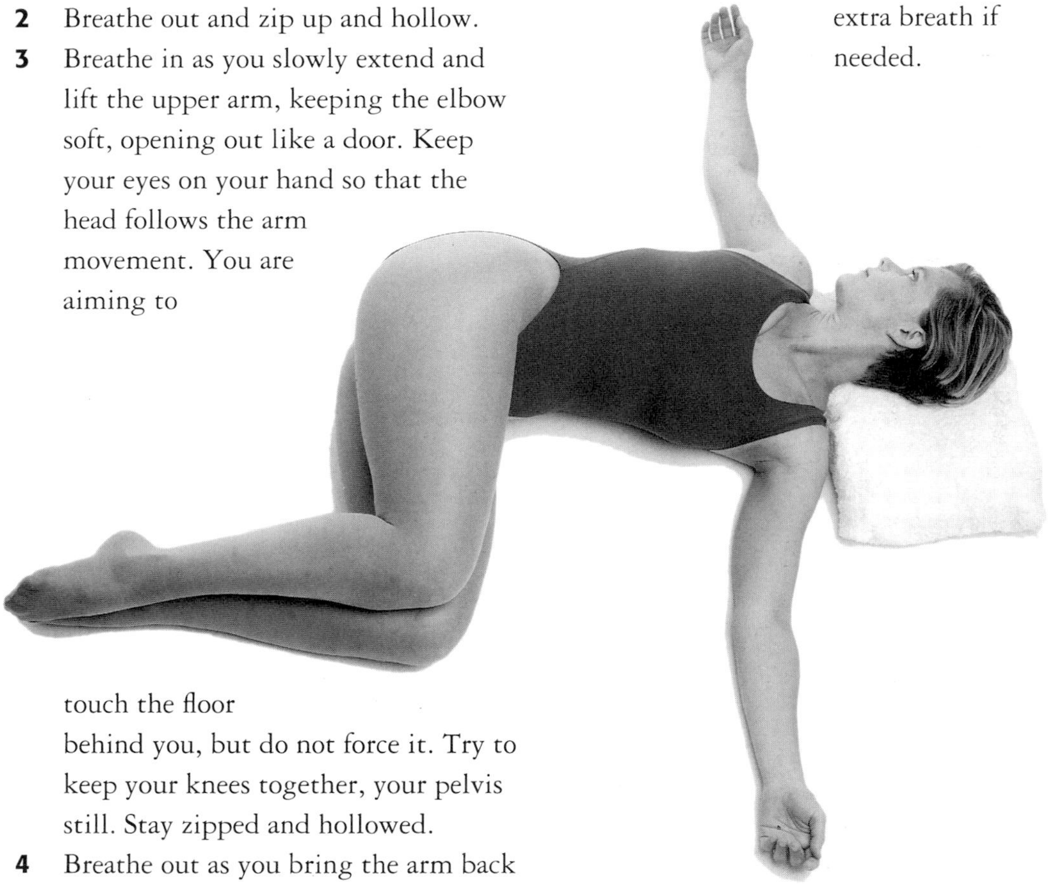

Watchpoints

▷ Keep hollowing throughout.

▷ Keep your knees glued together and on the floor.

▷ Don't forget to allow your head to roll naturally with the movement, making sure that it is supported by the pillow.

▷ You may take an extra breath if needed.

Relaxation

At last! The perfect way to end the day or the session. Ideally, you should persuade a friend to read the instructions to you. Otherwise, try taping them.

▷ Lie in the Relaxation Position (page 32).

▷ Allow your whole body to melt down into the floor.

▷ Allow your body to widen and lengthen.

▷ Take your awareness down to your feet.

▷ Soften the balls of the feet, uncurling the toes.

▷ Soften your ankles.

▷ Soften your calves.

▷ Release your knees.

▷ Release your thighs.

▷ Allow your hips to open.

▷ Allow the small of your back to sink into the floor as though you are sinking down into the folds of a hammock.

▷ Feel the length of your spine.

▷ Take your awareness down to your hands, stretch your fingers away from your palms, feel the centre of your palms opening.

▷ Then allow the fingers to curl, the palms to soften.

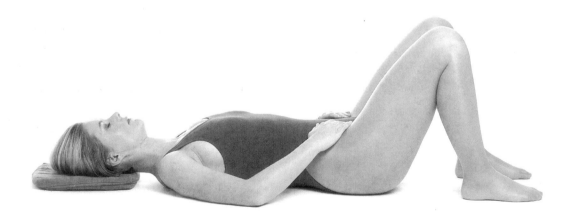

Relaxation position

- ▷ Allow your elbows to open.
- ▷ And the front of your shoulders to soften.
- ▷ With each out-breath allow your shoulder blades to widen.
- ▷ And your breastbone to soften.
- ▷ Allow your neck to release.
- ▷ Check your jaw, it should be loose and free.
- ▷ Allow your tongue to widen at its base and rest comfortably at the bottom of your mouth.
- ▷ Your lips are softly closed.
- ▷ Your eyes are softly closed.
- ▷ Your forehead is wide and smooth and completely free of lines.
- ▷ Your face feels soft.
- ▷ Your body is soft and warm.
- ▷ Your spine is gently released down into the floor.
- ▷ Observe your breathing, but do not interrupt it.
- ▷ Simply enjoy its natural rhythm . . .

To come out of the relaxation . . .

- ▷ Very gently allow your head to roll to one side. Just allow the weight of the head to take it over.
- ▷ Slowly bring the head back to the centre and allow it to roll to the other side . . . bring it back to the centre.
- ▷ Then wriggle your fingers.
- ▷ And then your toes.
- ▷ Very slowly, roll on to one side and rest there for a few minutes before slowly getting up . . .

Pilates has changed my life – this may sound a dramatic statement but as an actress who has suffered almost fifteen years of acute back pain, I am thrilled to be almost pain free. The disipline of Pilates is, I believe, excellent for people in professions like ours, where high levels of stress are often internalized.

Pilates is teaching me to re-educate the way I use my body, to isolate and strengthen muscles I'd forgotten I had, to realize the importance of stretching and opening up and above all to breathe correctly.

When taught as well as this it's brilliant.

Sally Knyvette

Working out the Pilates Way

Patience and persistence are vital qualities in the ultimate successful accomplishment of any worthwhile endeavour. Practice your exercises diligently with a fixed and unalterable determination that you will permit nothing else to sway you from keeping the faith with yourself.

Joseph Pilates

To help you to plan your exercise sessions, we have worked out a selection of daily, thrice weekly and twice weekly sessions from the exercises in this book. You can choose according to how much time you have available.

Following the plan, over the course of a week, will mean that you have given your body a complete workout using all the major muscle groups and perfectly balancing strength and flexibility exercises. Each session is also 'balanced' in its own right. Where an advanced exercise is recommended, we have given you an 'all levels' alternative.

You may use any of the Daily Workouts as warm-ups before sport or gym work.

Of course, if you have access to our other books on Pilates, *Body Control: The Pilates Way* and *The Mind–Body Workout*, or if you have one of our videos, you can add even more combinations of exercises!

Seven Daily Workouts (20–30 minutes each)

DAY ONE

DAY TWO

DAY THREE

Working Out Three Times a Week

Three balanced sessions of approximately one hour.

SESSION ONE

Working Out Twice a Week

Two balanced sessions of approximately 90 minutes.

SESSION ONE

Further Reading

On Pilates

Body Control: The Pilates Way Lynne
    Robinson and Gordon Thomson,
    Newleaf, 1997
The Mind–Body Workout Lynne Robinson
    and Helge Fisher, Pan Books, 1998
Morning Energizer: Pilates Through the Day
    Lynne Robinson, Pan Books, 1999
Desk Reviver: Pilates Through the Day Lynne
    Robinson, Pan Books, 1999
Evening Relaxer: Pilates Through the Day
    Lynne Robinson, Pan Books, 1999
Off to Sleep: Pilates Through the Day Lynne
    Robinson, Pan Books, 1999
How to Improve Your Posture Fran Lehen,
    Cornerstone Library, 1982
*The Pilates Method of Physical and Mental
    Conditioning* Philip Friedman and Gail
    Eisen, Warner Books, 1980
Every Body is Beautiful Ron Fletcher,
    Lippencott, 1978 (out of print)
Pilates: Return to Life Through Contrology
    J.H. Pilates and William J. Miller,
    Presentations Dynamics Inc, 1934
Your Health J.H. Pilates, Presentations
    Dynamics Inc, 1934

General

'Muscle Control – Pain Control. What
    exercises would you prescribe?' Article
    by C.A. Richardson and G.A. Jull,
    Department of Physiotherapy,
    University of Queensland, Australia.
    Manual Therapy, Pearson Professional
    Ltd., 1995

'Dysfunction of Tranversus Abdominus
    associated with Chronic Low Back
    Pain'. Article by P.W. Hodges,
    Department of Physiotherapy, The
    University of Queensland, Australia.
    MPAA Conference Proceedings, 1995

Manual of Structural Kinesiology Clem
    Thompson, Times Mirror/Mosby
    College Publishing, 1989

Anatomy of Movement Blandine Calais-
    Germain, Eastland Press 1993

The Anatomy Coloring Book Wynn Kapit
    and Lawrence M. Elson, HarperCollins
    Publishers, 1977

Inside Ballet Technique Valerie Grieg, Princeton Book Company, 1994

Dancing Longer, Dancing Stronger Andrea Watkins and Priscilla M. Clarkson, Princeton Book Company, 1990

Flexibility, Principles and Practice Christopher Norris, Black, 1994

Dance Kinesiology Sally Sevey Fitt, Schirmer, 1988

The Body Has Its Reasons: Anti-Exercises and Self-Awareness Therese Bertherat and Carol Bernstein, Cedar, 1988

Your Body, Biofeedback at its Best B.J. Jencks, NelsonHall, Chicago, 1977

The Art Of Changing – A New Approach to the Alexander Technique Glen Park, Ashgrove Press Ltd., 1989

Therapeutic Exercise Foundations and Techniques Carolyn Kisner and Lynn Allen Colby, F.A. Davis Company, 1990

Human Movement Potential – Its Ideokinetic Facilitation Lulu Swiegard, Harper and Row Publishers Inc., University Press of America Inc., 1974

Body Stories – A Guide To Experiential Anatomy Andrea Olsen, Station Hill Press, 1991

Body Fitness and Exercise – Basic Theory and Practice for Therapists Mo Rosser, Hodder and Stoughton, 1995

Sports Injuries – Diagnosis and Management for Physiotherapists Christopher Norris, Butterworth Heinemann, 1993

Muscle Testing and Function Kendall, Kendall and Wadsworth, Williams and Wilkins, Baltimore/London, 1971

Further Information

United Kingdom

A wide range of information can be found on the Body Control Pilates website at: *www.bodycontrol.co.uk*

Please send a stamped addressed envelope for a national listing of the Association's member teachers to:

The Body Control Pilates Association
17 Queensberry Mews West
South Kensington
London SW7 2DY
Pilates Information Line 0870 169 0000
(office hours)

Please write to BCPTT to request an Information Pack on teacher training courses in Pilates matwork and machine work.

Body Control Pilates Teacher Training
17 Queensberry Mews West
South Kensington
London SW7 2DY

For information on consumer and specialist workshops, corporate programmes, studio and home equipment and books and videos, please contact:

Body Control Pilates Limited
PO Box 238
Tonbridge
Kent TN11 8ZL
Pilates Information Line 01753 655 500
(office hours)

Mail order supply of specially commissioned clothing ideal both for Pilates and for general leisure wear:

Body Control Clothing Limited
1 Cross Street
Market Harborough
Leicestershire LE16 9ES
Tel: 01858 469588

The following organizations may also be useful:

Osteopathic Information Service
PO Box 2074, Reading, Berkshire
RG1 4YR

Chartered Society of Physiotherapists
14 Bedford Row, London, WC1R 4ED

The Exercise Association of England
Limited
Unit 4, Angel Gate, 326 City Road,
London EC1V 2PT

The National Back Pain Association
16 Elmtree Road, Teddington, Middlesex
TW11 8ST

Overseas

Balanced Body.
7500 14th Avenue, Suite 23, Sacramento,
CA 95820–3539, USA

The Physicalmind Institute
1807 Second Street # 28 , Santa Fe, New
Mexico 87501, USA

The Australian Pilates Method Association
PO Box 27, Mosman, NSW 2088,
Australia

Pilates Body Control
Suite 151, Private Bag X3036,
Postnet Paarl 7620, South Africa

Body Studio
2/141 Wellesley Street West
Victoria Square
Auckland, New Zealand

These fantastic Pilates books are all available from your local bookshop, or by sending a cheque or postal order as detailed on last page.

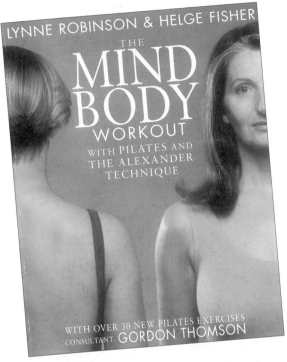

Mind–Body Workout
0 330 36946 6 £12.99 pb

A fresh approach to exercise combining Pilates and the Alexander Technique

Body Control – The Pilates Way
0 330 36945 8 £7.99 pb

The original best–selling manual taking Pilates out of the studio and into the home

Pilates Through the Day

A series of mini-books to help your body make the most of every day.

The Morning Energizer
0 330 37327 7 £2.99 pb

The Evening Relaxer
0 330 37329 3 £2.99 pb

The Desk Reviver
0 330 37328 5 £2.99 pb

Off to Sleep
0 330 37330 7 £2.99 pb

Books available from all good bookshops, or from
Book Services By Post, PO Box 29, Douglas, Isle of Man IM99 1BQ.
Credit card hotline 01624 675137. Postage and packing free.

Lynne Robinson's expert tuition, in association with Fitness Consultant Gordon Thomson, is now available on two Telstar videos, **BODY CONTROL THE PILATES WAY** and **PILATES WEEKLY WORKOUT**. Both are priced at £12.99 and are available at all good video stockists.

Regular information updates appear on the Body Control Pilates website at **www.bodycontrol.co.uk**